PYONGYANG

D1465105

PYONGYANG

A JOURNEY IN NORTH KOREA

GUY DELISLE

JONATHAN CAPE
LONDON

Published by Jonathan Cape 2006

4 6 8 10 9 7 5

Entire contents copyright © 2003, 2005 by Guy Delisle and L'Association
Translation copyright © 2005, 2006 by Helge Dascher

Originally published in France by L'Association
L'Association

First English-language edition published in Canada by Drawn & Quarterly

Translation copyright © 2005, 2006 by Helge Dascher

Hand-lettered by Dirk Rehm
Publication design: Guy Delisle and Tom Devlin

First published in Great Britain in 2006 by
Jonathan Cape
Random House, 20 Vauxhall Bridge Road,
London SW1V 2SA

Random House Australia (Pty) Limited
20 Alfred Street, Milsons Point, Sydney,
New South Wales 2061, Australia

Random House New Zealand Limited
18 Poland Road, Glenfield,
Auckland 10, New Zealand

Random House (Pty) Limited
Isle of Houghton, Corner of Boundary Road & Carse O'Gowrie,
Houghton 2198, South Africa

Random House Publishers India Private Limited
301 World Trade Tower, Hotel Intercontinental Grand Complex,
Barakhamba Lane, New Delhi 110 001, India

The Random House Group Limited Reg. No. 954009
www.randomhouse.co.uk

A CIP catalogue record for this book
is available from the British Library

ISBN 9780224079907 (from Jan 2007)
ISBN 0224079905

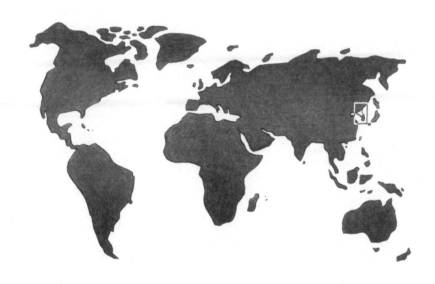

NORTH KOREA

PYONGYANG

SEOUL

SOUTH KOREA

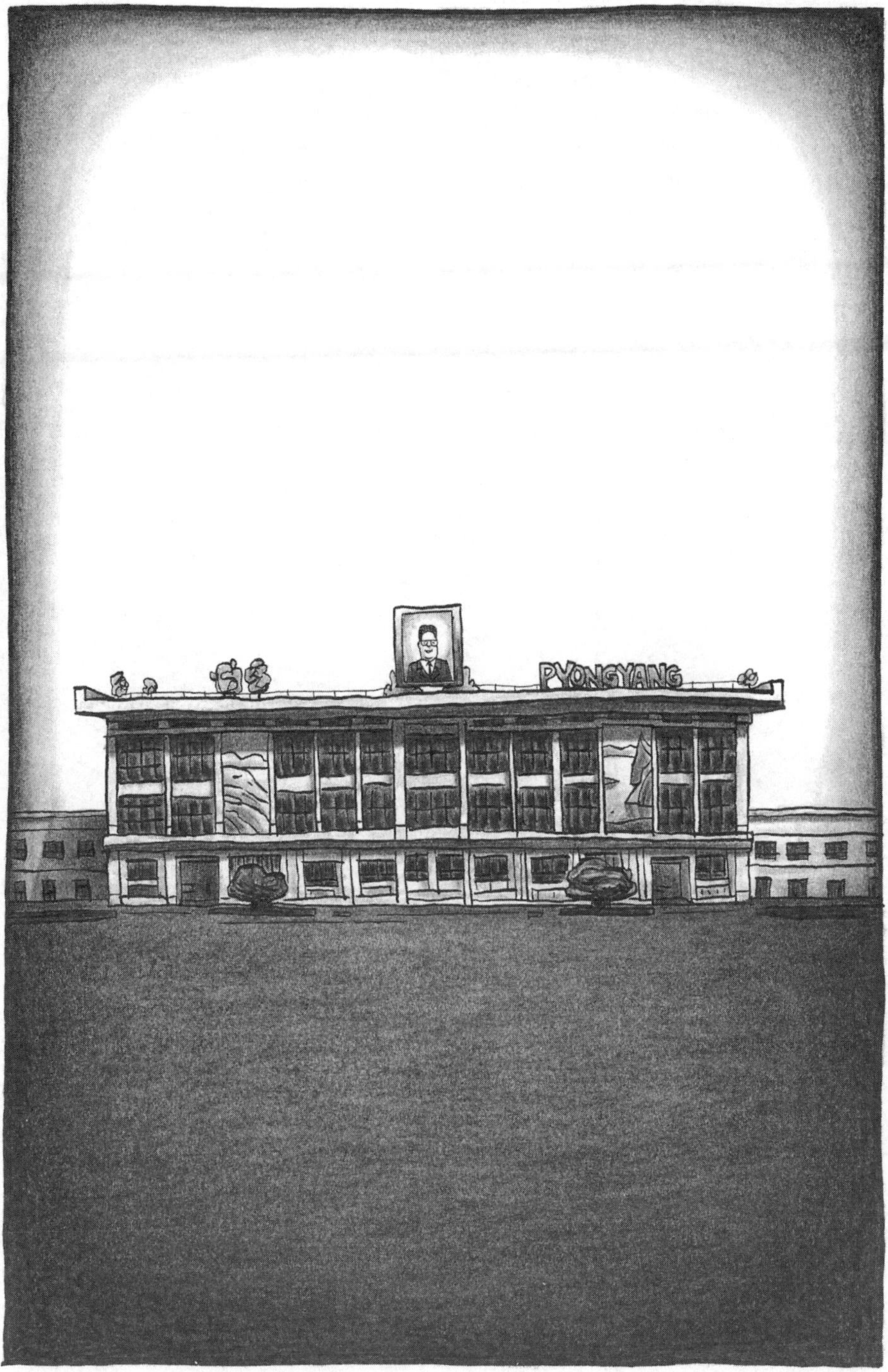
PYONGYANG

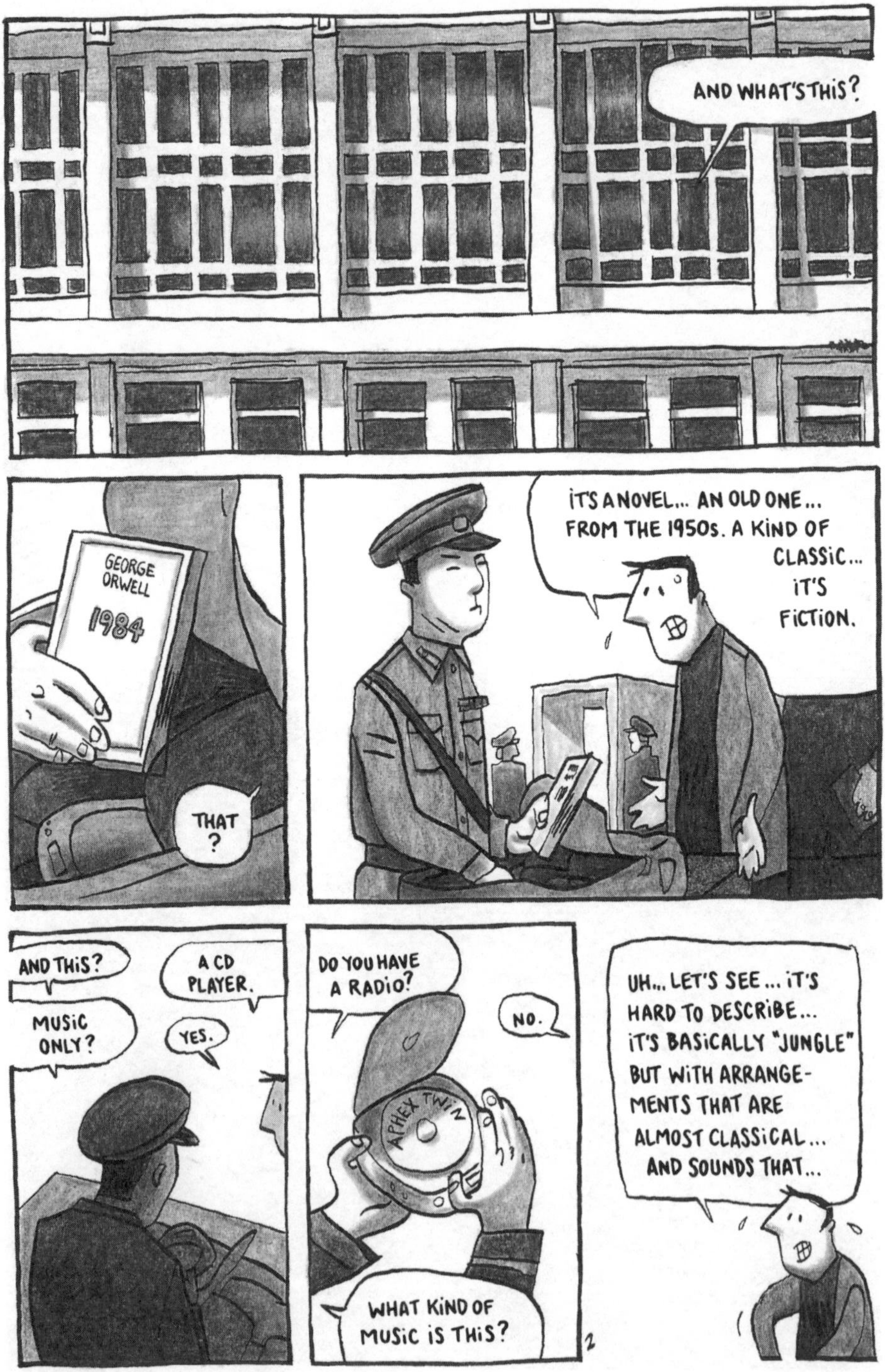
AND WHAT'S THIS?
GEORGE ORWELL
1984
THAT?
IT'S A NOVEL... AN OLD ONE... FROM THE 1950s. A KIND OF CLASSIC... IT'S FICTION.
AND THIS?
A CD PLAYER.
MUSIC ONLY?
YES.
DO YOU HAVE A RADIO?
NO.
APHEX TWIN
WHAT KIND OF MUSIC IS THIS?
UH... LET'S SEE... IT'S HARD TO DESCRIBE... IT'S BASICALLY "JUNGLE" BUT WITH ARRANGE-MENTS THAT ARE ALMOST CLASSICAL... AND SOUNDS THAT...

YOU'RE HERE FOR THE SEK?

IF THAT'S THE NAME OF THE ANIMATION STUDIO, YES...

OH! WELL, EVERYTHING IS ALL RIGHT THEN.

OUR APOLOGIES!

MISTER GUY?

 I'M MR. KYU, YOUR GUIDE.

 A PLEASURE.

THE DRIVER IS OUTSIDE.

I CAN BARELY MAKE OUT HIS FACE BECAUSE THERE'S NO LIGHT IN THE AIRPORT.

3

THE DRIVER HANDS ME FLOWERS THAT I KNOW AREN'T REALLY MEANT FOR ME.

TO HELP ME PREPARE FOR THIS TRIP, I WAS GIVEN A BOOKLET OF TRAVEL TIPS.

THANKS.

HOW NICE.

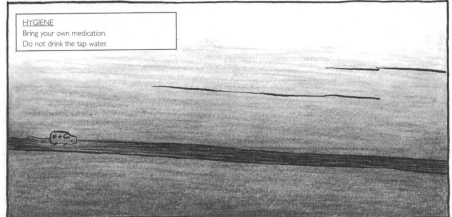

HYGIENE
Bring your own medication.
Do not drink the tap water.

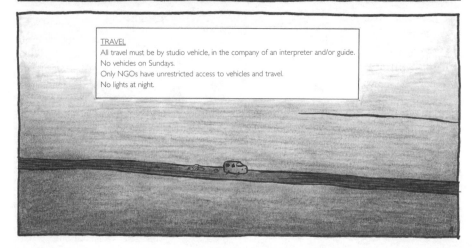

TRAVEL
All travel must be by studio vehicle, in the company of an interpreter and/or guide.
No vehicles on Sundays.
Only NGOs have unrestricted access to vehicles and travel.
No lights at night.

ALLOWED
Audio cassettes.
CD player and CDs.
Portable computer and printer.
Cameras and film, camcorder. Not everything can be photographed.
Food: mustard, ketchup, etc.
Books to give to interpreter at the end of the trip.

PROHIBITED
Mobile phone (confiscated at airport and returned
on departure.)
Pornography.

iNCREDiBLE! HE'S SMOKING
iN AN AiR-CONDiTiONED CAR
WiTH CLOSED WiNDOWS!

GREAT.

I CAN'T BREATHE
AND I'M COLD.

MY GUIDE SUGGESTS WE VISIT THE HIGHEST POINT IN THE CITY TO ADMIRE THE VIEW BEFORE GOING TO THE HOTEL.

AN ELEGANT WAY OF TAKING ME ON A STOP THAT'S OBLIGATORY FOR NEWCOMERS WITHOUT BEING OBVIOUS.

6

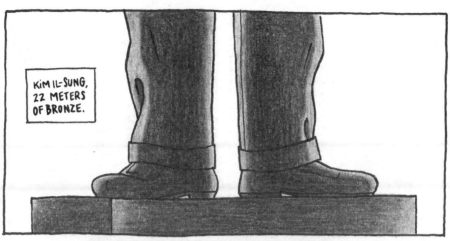

KIM IL-SUNG, 22 METERS OF BRONZE.

FOR VISITORS, IT'S A DISPROPORTIONATE ONE-ON-ONE WITH THE GIGANTIC FIGURE OF THE FATHER OF THE NATION.

WHO, DESPITE HIS DEATH (1912-1994), IS STILL PRESIDENT.

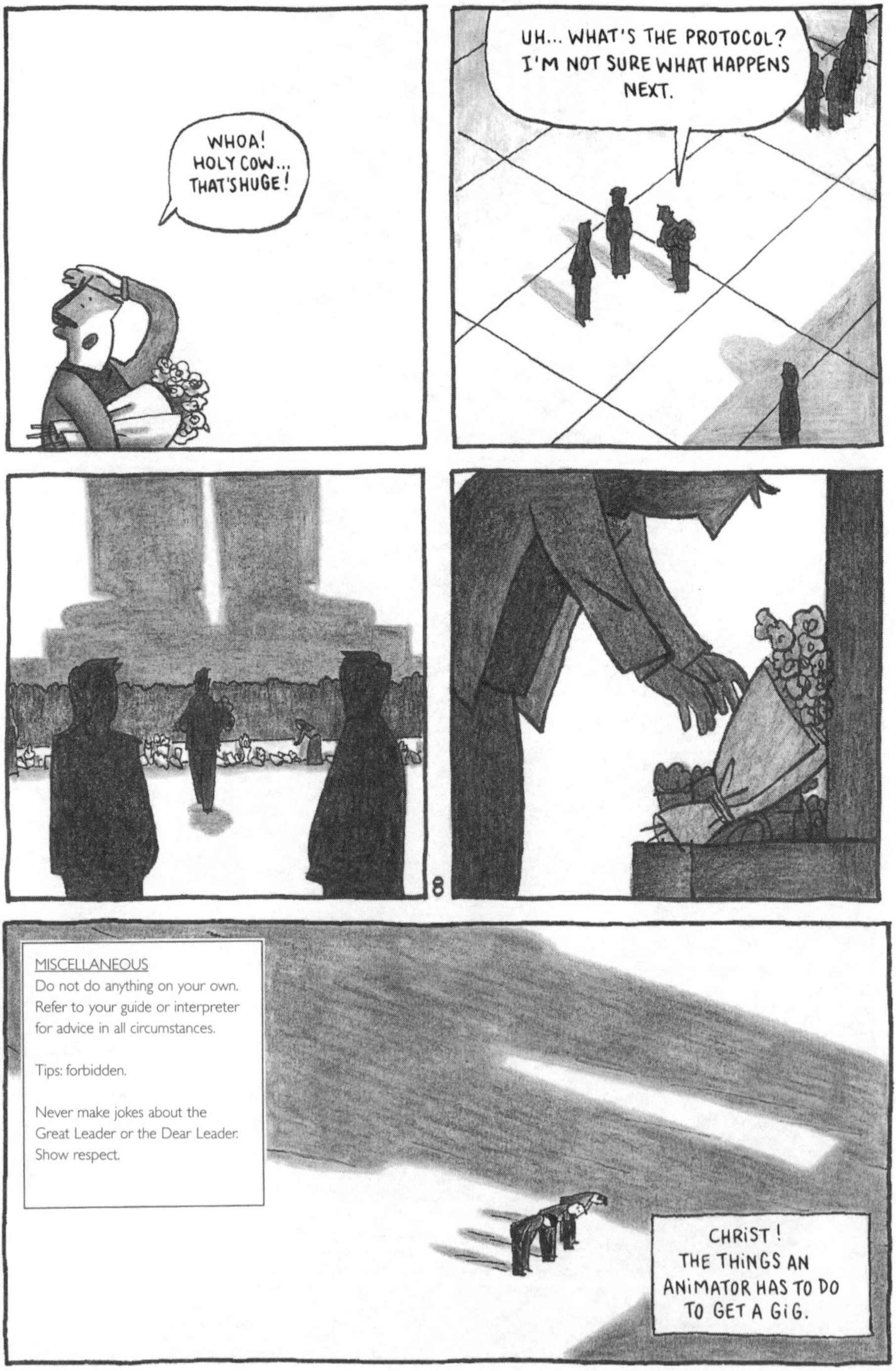
WHOA! HOLY COW... THAT'S HUGE!
UH... WHAT'S THE PROTOCOL? I'M NOT SURE WHAT HAPPENS NEXT.
MISCELLANEOUS
Do not do anything on your own. Refer to your guide or interpreter for advice in all circumstances.
Tips: forbidden.
Never make jokes about the Great Leader or the Dear Leader. Show respect.
CHRIST! THE THINGS AN ANIMATOR HAS TO DO TO GET A GIG.

BACK IN THE PARKING LOT, I COME ACROSS ALL THE FOREIGNERS WHO WERE ON THE FLIGHT, ALONG WITH THEIR RESPECTIVE GUIDES.

GERMAN MINERAL WATER EXPORTER.

FRENCH ALCATEL EMPLOYEE.

YOUNG ITALIAN FOREIGN AID WORKER.

DURING MY STAY, I MET EVERY ONE OF THEM AGAIN.

MY HOTEL IS ON A SMALL ISLAND, NOT FAR FROM DOWNTOWN.

IT'S GOT THOSE GOOD OLD STANDARD ROOMS—COLD AND IMPERSONAL, JUST LIKE THEY LIKE THEM IN ASIA.

9

NORTH KOREA IS THE WORLD'S MOST ISOLATED COUNTRY. FOREIGNERS TRICKLE IN. THERE'S NO INTERNET. THERE ARE NO CAFÉS. IN FACT, THERE'S NO ENTERTAINMENT. IT'S HARD TO EVEN LEAVE THE HOTEL AND MEETING KOREANS IS NEXT TO IMPOSSIBLE.

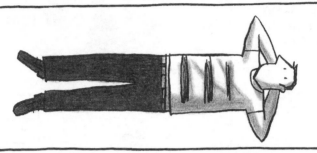

LUCKILY I'VE HAD PRACTICE BEING ALONE BECAUSE THIS WON'T BE A FUNHOUSE.

WELL, THAT'S WHAT I THOUGHT, BUT I WAS WRONG—WHICH JUST GOES TO SHOW THAT YOU'VE GOT TO BE READY FOR ANYTHING WHEN YOU TRAVEL.

KNOCK KNOCK

MISTER GUY? READY TO GO TO THE STUDIO?

HEY, ISN'T THAT KARL UP THERE?

YOU KNOW MARX? VERY GOOD.

A BIT... DOESN'T EVERYBODY?

OH NO, NOT MANY CAPITALISTS DO.

REALLY.

THE STUDIO MIGHT HAVE BEEN INTENDED TO EDUCATE THE MASSES, BUT THESE DAYS IT'S USED TO ATTRACT FOREIGN CURRENCY, MOST OF IT FRENCH.

HELLO!

THERE YOU ARE!

I FIND THE PERSON I'VE COME TO REPLACE: SANDRINE, SOMEONE I OFTEN CROSS PATHS WITH IN THE SMALL WORLD OF ANIMATION.

Pfff.

Fed up.

SO, FIRST SAIGON AND NOW PYONGYANG, HA HA HA HA!

YEEEAH!

THE LAST TIME WE MET WAS IN VIETNAM. BEFORE THAT WAS PARIS AND OVER TEN YEARS AGO, THE SOUTH OF FRANCE.

AND THEN I'M QUITTING.

30? I DON'T KNOW.

SOUNDS LIKE THEY'RE GOING UNDER.

BLAH

BLAH

I'VE HAD IT WITH PARIS...

BLAH

SO WHAT'S HE UP TO NOW?

BLAH

THEY EVEN DO THE LAYOUT THERE.

BLAH

BLAH BLAH

BLAH BLAH

1 2

OK, LET'S GET STARTED.

I'M DOING CORRECTIONS ON EPISODE ONE.

BLAH

BLAH

OH, YES, RIGHT... I FORGOT.

I'VE COME HERE TO WORK.

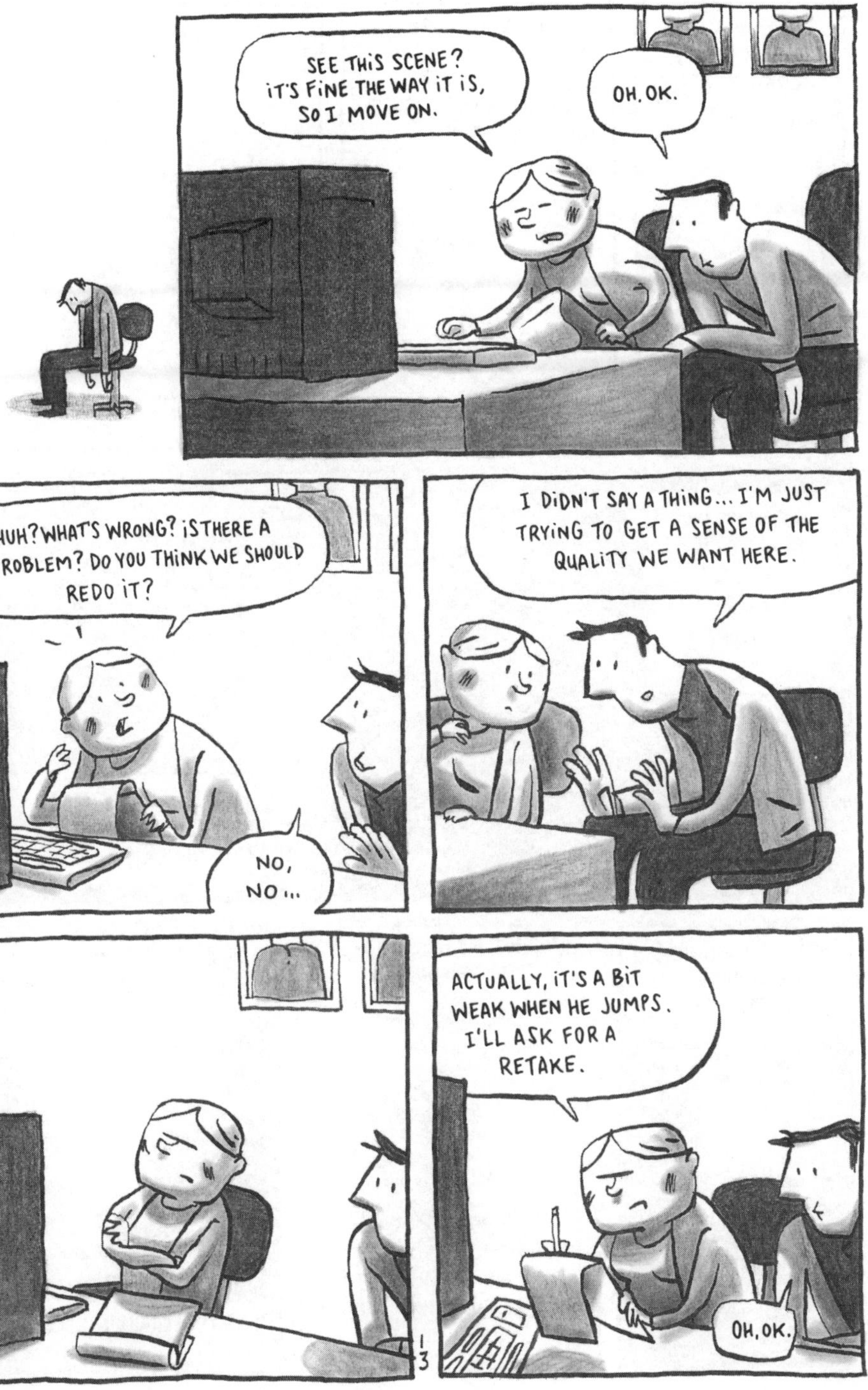
SEE THIS SCENE? IT'S FINE THE WAY IT IS, SO I MOVE ON.
OH, OK.
HUH? WHAT'S WRONG? IS THERE A PROBLEM? DO YOU THINK WE SHOULD REDO IT?
NO, NO...
I DIDN'T SAY A THING... I'M JUST TRYING TO GET A SENSE OF THE QUALITY WE WANT HERE.
ACTUALLY, IT'S A BIT WEAK WHEN HE JUMPS. I'LL ASK FOR A RETAKE.
OH, OK.

WANNA HAVE A DRINK?

RICHARD, WHO WORKS TWO FLOORS UP FOR ELLIPSE (ANOTHER FRENCH STUDIO), SUGGESTS WE TAKE A BREAK.

A DRINK! ... WHERE?

WE WIND UP NEARBY, IN WHAT LOOKS LIKE A HOTEL.

EXCEPT FOR A FEW SOLDIERS, THE PLACE IS DESERTED.

WE SIT DOWN NEXT TO THE WINDOW TO HAVE SOME LIGHT.

SHIT, WE FORGOT TO TELL THE GUARDS ...

AFTER 3 MONTHS IN NORTH KOREA, SANDRINE HAS DEVELOPED CERTAIN REFLEXES.

14

WHO CARES? WE'RE RIGHT NEXT DOOR.

THIS IS RICHARD'S SECOND WEEK.

I HOPE THINGS GO BETTER HERE...

OUR COLLEAGUE HAS COME TO WORK ON CORTO MALTESE.

· CORTO MALTESE ·

MONUMENT OF THE 9th ART

©CASTERMAN-PRATT

SEOUL WAS A HUGE WASTE OF TIME...

IN FACT, THEY HAD TO LEAVE WITH THE SCENES AND REDO EVERYTHING IN PARIS.

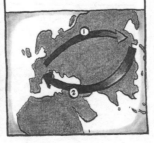

BUT SINCE WE'VE RUN OUT OF CASH...

...THEY'RE WRAPPING UP PRODUCTION IN PYONGYANG.

ALL WE'RE DOING HERE ARE THE INBETWEENS ...

REALLY?

15

MINI GLOSSARY

KEYS: DRAWN BY <u>ANIMATORS</u> IN PARIS.

INBETWEENS: TO BE DRAWN BY <u>ASSISTANTS</u> IN NORTH KOREA.

QUIZ: Which of these are key frames?

Answer: 1, 4, 8

HENCE THE TRIED AND TRUE FORMULA.

GREAT, THAT WAY KIDS DON'T HAVE TO BOTHER READING THE BOOKS. THEY'LL JUST THINK EVERY-THING STARTED ON TV, LIKE TINTIN.

MMM.

RICHARD'S GUIDE TURNS UP. HE LOOKS RELIEVED TO SEE US.

SANDRINE AND I DECIDE THAT WE WANT TO WALK BACK TO THE HOTEL.

OUR GUIDES DON'T ACTUALLY OBJECT, BUT THEY'RE NOT HAPPY, EITHER.

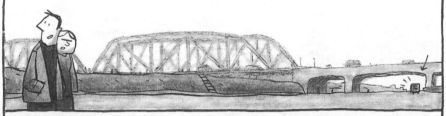

ARE THEY FOLLOWING?

NOPE, I DON'T SEE THEM.

WELL, COOL... THEY'RE NOT SUCH A PAIN AFTER ALL.

A MOMENT LATER, WE FIGURED OUT THEIR SYSTEM: THEY WERE WAITING FOR US DOWN THE ROAD, AND WHEN WE CAUGHT UP THEY ADVANCED AGAIN, ALL THE WAY TO THE HOTEL.

FORGING AHEAD INTO THE 21st CENTURY!

PYONGYANG HAS THREE HOTELS FOR FOREIGNERS.

EACH HAS ITS ADVANTAGES.

THE POTONGGANG, WITH ITS CABLE TV (CNN).

THE KORYO, IN THE HEART OF TOWN.

THE YANGAKKDO, WHERE SANRINE AND I ARE STAYING.

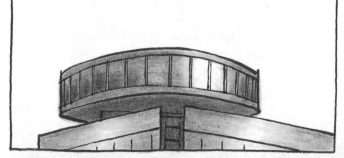

IT'S A MASSIVE 50-STOREY TOWER WITH A REVOLVING RESTAURANT, BUILT IN THE 1980s BY A FRENCH FIRM.

THAT EXPLAINS THE FRENCH DESIGNER TOILETS.

AAAH! VIVE LA FRANCE.

ALL FOREIGNERS ARE ON THE 15th FLOOR, THE ONLY ONE THAT'S LIT.

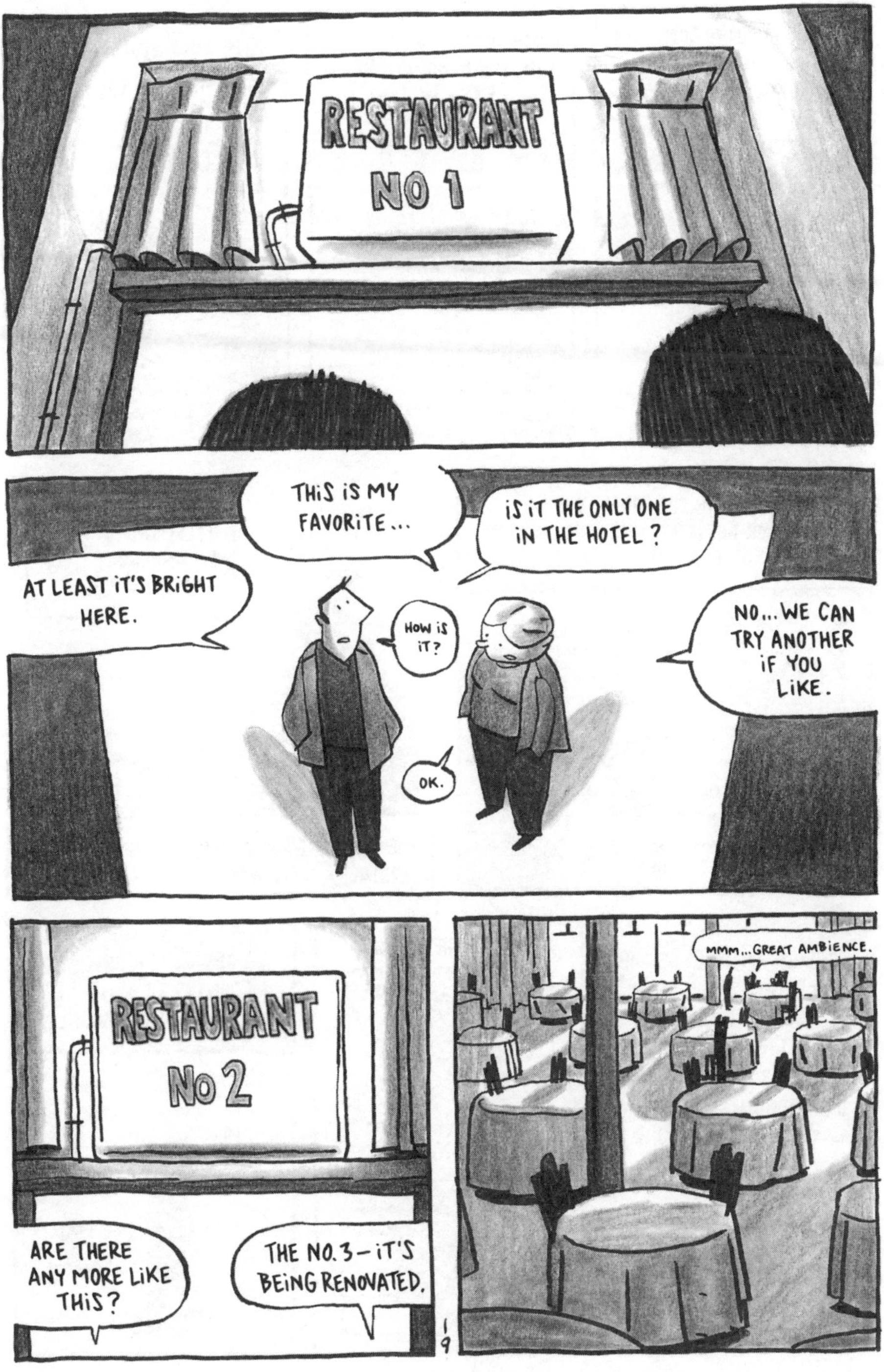
RESTAURANT
NO 1
AT LEAST IT'S BRIGHT HERE.
THIS IS MY FAVORITE...
IS IT THE ONLY ONE IN THE HOTEL ?
HOW IS IT?
NO... WE CAN TRY ANOTHER IF YOU LIKE.
OK.
RESTAURANT
No 2
ARE THERE ANY MORE LIKE THIS?
THE NO. 3 – IT'S BEING RENOVATED.
MMM... GREAT AMBIENCE.

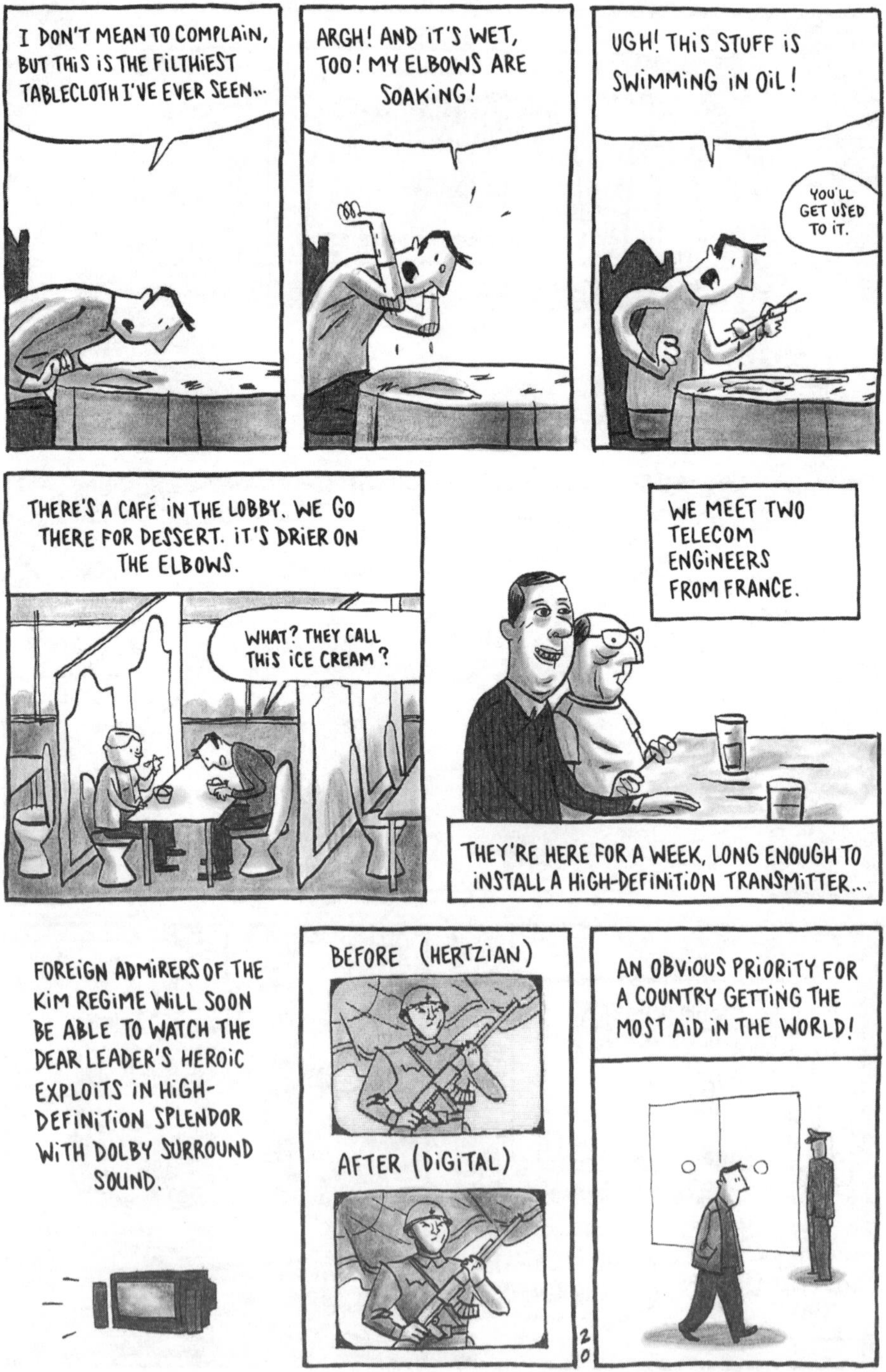
I DON'T MEAN TO COMPLAIN, BUT THIS IS THE FILTHIEST TABLECLOTH I'VE EVER SEEN...
ARGH! AND IT'S WET, TOO! MY ELBOWS ARE SOAKING!
UGH! THIS STUFF IS SWIMMING IN OIL!
YOU'LL GET USED TO IT.
THERE'S A CAFÉ IN THE LOBBY. WE GO THERE FOR DESSERT. IT'S DRIER ON THE ELBOWS.
WHAT? THEY CALL THIS ICE CREAM?
WE MEET TWO TELECOM ENGINEERS FROM FRANCE.
THEY'RE HERE FOR A WEEK, LONG ENOUGH TO INSTALL A HIGH-DEFINITION TRANSMITTER...
FOREIGN ADMIRERS OF THE KIM REGIME WILL SOON BE ABLE TO WATCH THE DEAR LEADER'S HEROIC EXPLOITS IN HIGH-DEFINITION SPLENDOR WITH DOLBY SURROUND SOUND.
BEFORE (HERTZIAN)
AFTER (DIGITAL)
AN OBVIOUS PRIORITY FOR A COUNTRY GETTING THE MOST AID IN THE WORLD!

IN THE MIDDLE OF THE NIGHT, I WATCH A PERSON WHO'S WALKING BACKWARDS. I DON'T KNOW IF IT'S THE JET LAG OR THE FACT THAT I'M BRACED FOR ANYTHING HERE, BUT THE SIGHT DOESN'T SEEM ABNORMAL OR EVEN SURPRISING.

OH, LOOK, A GUY WALKING BACKWARDS.

THE BEST THING ABOUT LIVING IN HOTELS IS LYING DOWN ON THE BEDSPREAD WITH YOUR SHOES ON.

HERE I AM, BREAKING A MAJOR FAMILY TABOO BEFORE YOUR EYES.

IT'S BLISS.

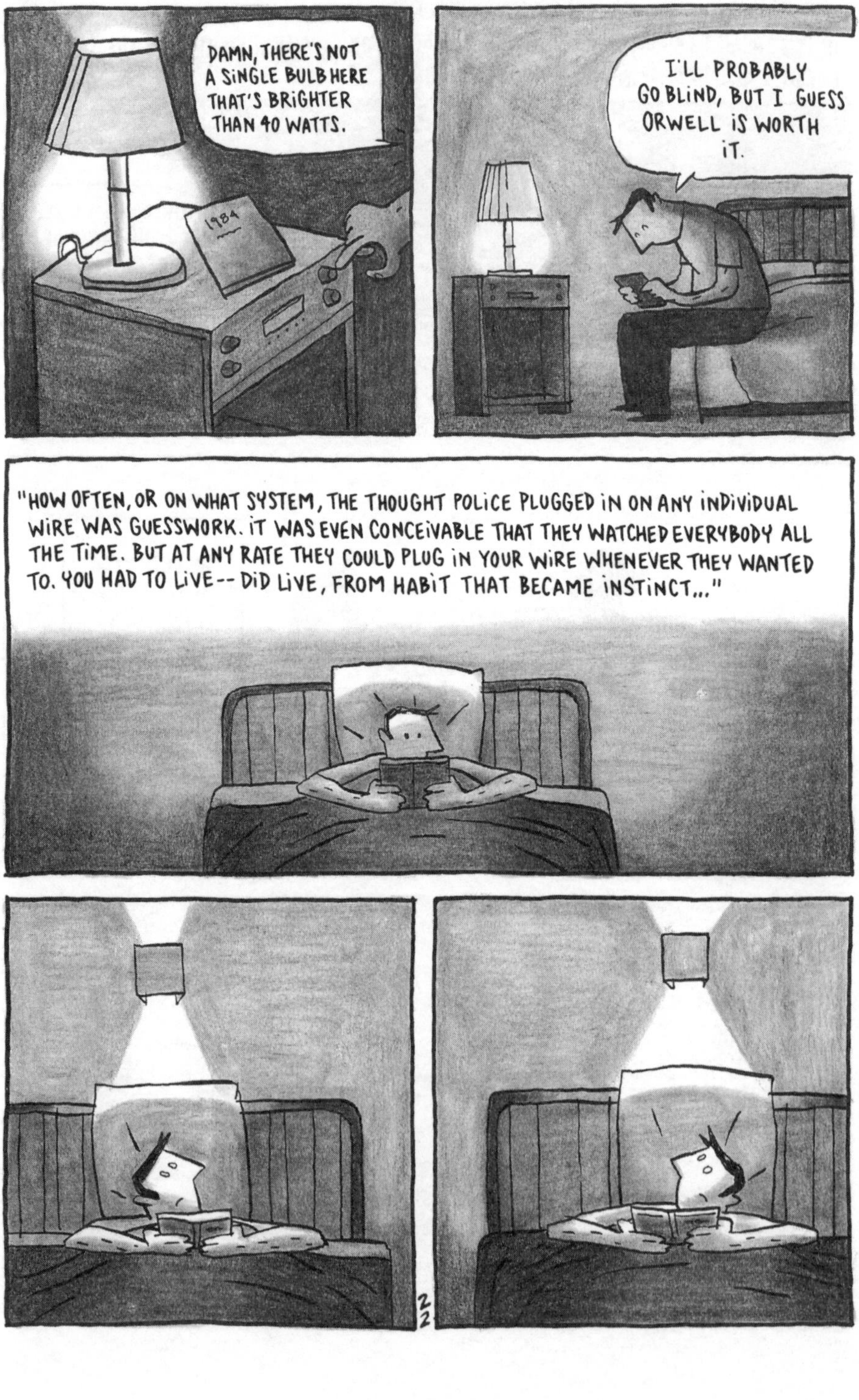
DAMN, THERE'S NOT A SINGLE BULB HERE THAT'S BRIGHTER THAN 40 WATTS.
1984
I'LL PROBABLY GO BLIND, BUT I GUESS ORWELL IS WORTH IT.
"HOW OFTEN, OR ON WHAT SYSTEM, THE THOUGHT POLICE PLUGGED IN ON ANY INDIVIDUAL WIRE WAS GUESSWORK. IT WAS EVEN CONCEIVABLE THAT THEY WATCHED EVERYBODY ALL THE TIME. BUT AT ANY RATE THEY COULD PLUG IN YOUR WIRE WHENEVER THEY WANTED TO. YOU HAD TO LIVE-- DID LIVE, FROM HABIT THAT BECAME INSTINCT..."

THE MORNING FOG OVER TAEDONG STRETCHES TO INFINITY IN THE DISTANCE. MUNICIPAL LOUDSPEAKERS INTONE THEIR LITANY.

THERE'S A POEM IN THE AIR.

HEY! I KNOW, I'LL TALK IN RHYME ALL DAY... WHAT A GREAT IDEA...

HA HA!

AH, SCREW THAT. WHY DRIVE MYSELF NUTS ALL DAY MAKING UP RHYMES.

FORGET IT.

I JOIN SANDRINE AT THE FAR TABLE.

DID YOU SEE? THERE'S MELON TODAY.

OH RIGHT.

LOOK, THERE'S A BUNCH OF CHINESE DOING THE "REVERSE".

THE WHAT?

THEY'RE WALKING BACKWARDS. DIDN'T YOU KNOW? IT'S A TRADITIONAL FORM OF EXCERCISE.

OH, SO THAT'S IT.

AS USUAL, THE VAN, DRIVER, GUIDE AND TRANSLATOR ARE WAITING TO TAKE US TO THE STUDIO.

24

PYONGYANG : PHANTOM CITY IN A HERMIT NATION.

THE FEW DISMAL PICTURES YOU SEE IN THE WEST HAD ACTUALLY LED ME TO EXPECT WORSE.

TRAMWAYS, CARS, BUSES, TRUCKS... IT TURNS OUT THE STREETS AREN'T DESERTED AFTER ALL.

EVERYTHING IS VERY CLEAN. TOO CLEAN, IN FACT.

NO ONE LINGERS IN THE STREETS. EVERYONE HAS SOMEWHERE TO BE, SOMETHING TO DO.

NO LOITERING, NO OLD FOLKS CHATTING. TOTAL STERILITY.

IT'S ALL NEW.

DURING THE KOREAN WAR, BOMBS RAINED ON THE CITY FOR 3 YEARS, FLATTENING IT.

AFTERWARD, THE PARTY OBLITERATED ANYTHING RESEMBLING AN OPPOSITION...

AND SEALED OFF THE COUNTRY TO ALL SIDES.

THE CITY WAS ENTIRELY REBUILT ACCORDING TO THE GREAT LEADER'S PLANS.

AND THIS, AND...

WHOA! MORE THAN 90% OF THE SCENES HAVE TO BE REDONE.

I KNOW. WE HAD A LOUSY TEAM ON EPISODE 2.

OH.

OK, MARK UP THE REST AND I'LL GO CHECK THE RETAKES.

SURE.

TO CHECK THE ANIMATION, I WORK ON A COMPUTER THAT'S USED FOR PRODUCTION THE REST OF THE TIME.

WITH IT, I'VE INHERITED A TECHNICIAN WHO HELPS OUT WITH GREAT ZEAL INSTEAD OF TAKING A BREAK WHILE I DO MY STUFF.

WHENEVER I HESITATE...

UH...

SHE POINTS AT THE SPOT I'VE GOT TO CLICK.

IT GETS TO BE ANNOYING.

AFTER A WHILE, SHE LETS UP AND DECIDES TO GIVE ME A TASTE OF HER COUNTRY'S MUSICAL GENIUS INSTEAD.

THE TUNES SOUND LIKE A CROSS BETWEEN A NATIONAL ANTHEM AND THE THEME SONG OF A CHILDREN'S SHOW... LIKE A BARNEY REMIX OF "GOD SAVE THE QUEEN" OR "OH CANADA".

MY NEW FRIEND IS JUST SINGING RIGHT ALONG, LOOKING MY WAY TO GET ME GOING, TOO.

IN EVERY ROOM, ON EVERY FLOOR, IN EVERY BUILDING THROUGHOUT NORTH KOREA, PORTRAITS OF PAPA KIM AND HIS SON HANG SIDE BY SIDE ON ONE WALL.

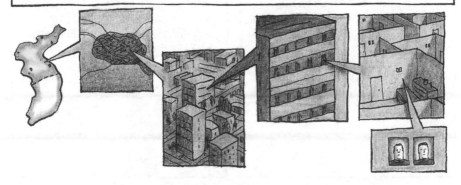

EXCEPT IN THE SHITTERS, OF COURSE.

AND SINCE "KIM IL SUNG IS KIM JONG-IL AND KIM JONG-IL IS KIM IL-SUNG", THEY'RE MADE TO LOOK ALIKE.

KIM SENIOR'S GRAY HAIR AND DEFORMING NECK TUMOR ARE GONE.

AS ARE KIM JUNIOR'S GLASSES AND EXCESS WEIGHT.

SAME SIZE, SAME AGE, SAME SUIT.

THAT WAY NOTHING EVER CHANGES — IT'S ALWAYS THE SAME HEAD AT THE HELM.

THE WORLD'S ONLY COMMUNIST DYNASTY.

HUH.

MY COFFEE BREAKS LEAD TO A FEW MORE OBSERVATIONS.

2/9

THE PORTRAITS, WHICH ARE HUNG HIGH ON THE WALLS, HAVE A WIDER EDGE ABOVE THAN BELOW.

THE ANGLE CUTS OUT ANY REFLECTIONS THAT COULD PREVENT YOU FROM CONTEMPLATING THE SUN OF THE 21st CENTURY AND HIS VENERABLE FATHER. IT ALSO INTENSIFIES THE GAZE IN THIS FACE-TO-FACE ENCOUNTER.

THERE'S A DETAIL ORWELL WOULD HAVE LIKED.

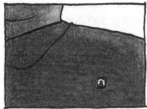

BOTH WEAR ONE OF THE OFFICIAL BADGES THAT INVARIABLY DEPICT KIM JUNIOR OR KIM SENIOR. YOU CAN'T TELL FROM THE PORTRAITS, BUT IT'S TEMPTING TO THINK THEY'RE WEARING EACH OTHER'S IMAGES, CREATING THE KIND OF SHORT CIRCUIT ANIMATORS LOVE...

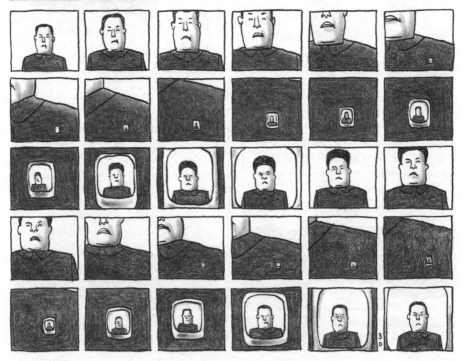

SCENE (117): When the character pulls on the ribbon, keep it tight as the bow unravels.

Or else he looks like he's holding a snake and playing with it.

Hmpf.

MISTER GUY.

AFTER ASKING TWO DAYS AGO, I'M BEING TAKEN TO VISIT ONE OF THE PRIDES OF THE NATION...

THE PYONG-YANG SUBWAY.

BURIED 90 METERS UNDERGROUND, THE PYONGYANG SUBWAY CAN DOUBLE AS A BOMB SHELTER IN CASE OF NUCLEAR ATTACK. WHAT BETTER WAY TO CULTIVATE A CONSTANT SENSE OF THREAT?

3/1

THE

LONG

WAY

DOWN.

A REGULAR.

MARBLE FLOORS, CHANDELIERS, SCULPTED COLUMNS. IT'S A SUBTERRANEAN PALACE TO THE GLORY OF PUBLIC TRANSIT.

EVERYWHERE, GARISH MURALS TRANSFIGURE A REALITY THAT JUST SEEMS DRAB TO ME.

IN A CITY WITHOUT ENOUGH ELECTRICITY TO POWER ITS TRAFFIC LIGHTS, THE SUBWAY TUNNELS ARE LIT UP LIKE LAS VEGAS!

STRANGE... VERRRY STRANGE...

THE TOUR ENDS AT THE NEXT STATION. OUR DRIVER PICKS US UP AT THE EXIT.

I'VE NEVER MET ANYONE WHO'S SEEN MORE THAN TWO STATIONS.

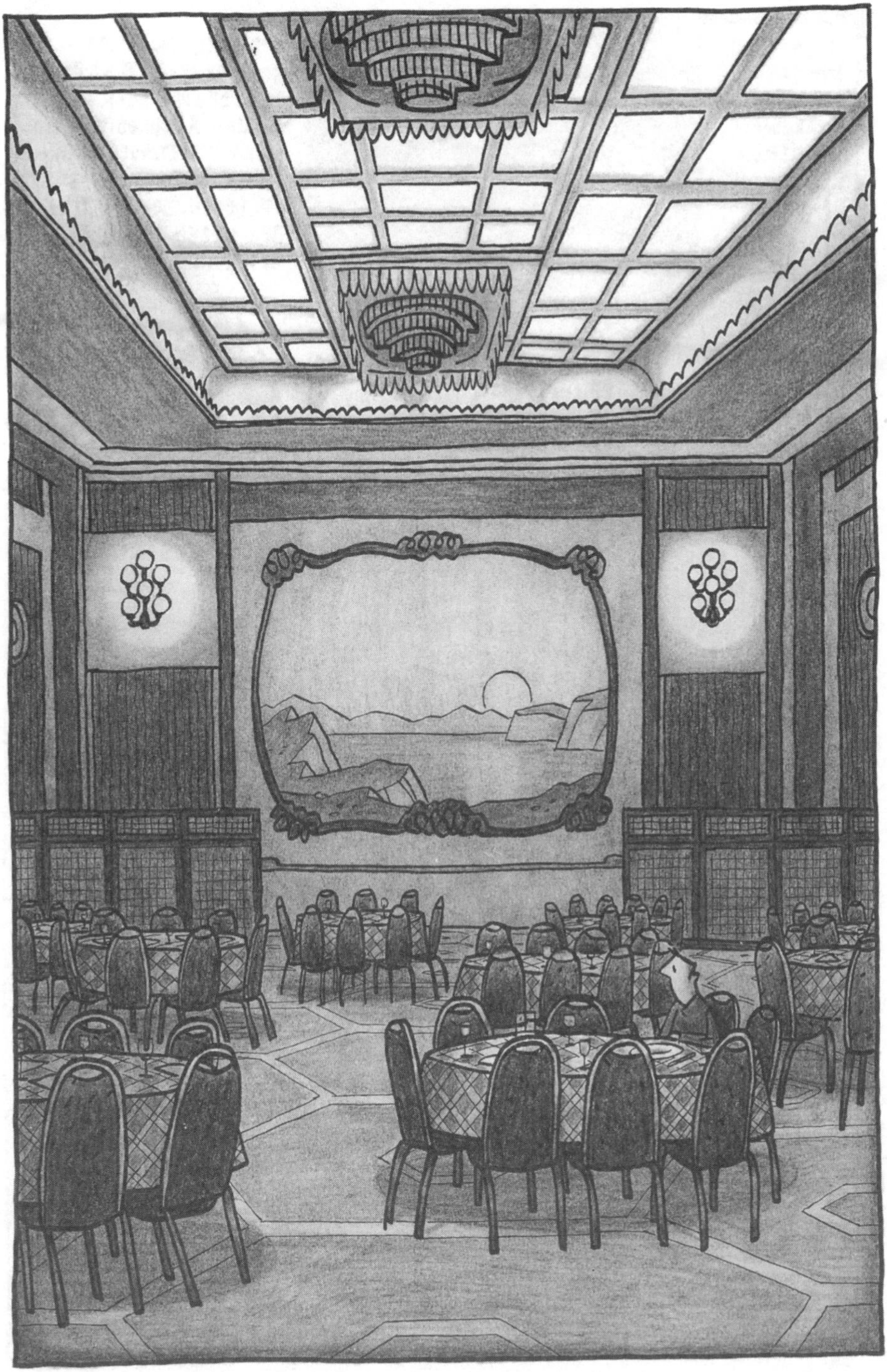

TO SAY GOOD-
BYE, SANDRINE
HAS ORGANIZED
A FAREWELL
DINNER IN
RESTAURANT
NO. 2...

IT'S QUICK AND EFFICIENT.
START OF MEAL: 8:30 P.M.
PILES OF FOOD, BEER ALL
AROUND, A FEW BOTTLES OF
RICE WINE, CONVERSATION,
BILL, END OF MEAL: 9:30 P.M.
WE LEAVE, SOME OF US
RED-NOSED AND OTHERS
RED-EARED.

... CHOSEN BY OUR KOREAN FRIENDS, PROBABLY FOR THE
PRIVACY THEY ENJOY IN A HOTEL FOR FOREIGNERS.

AS PART OF THE HAND-
OVER, I GET MY VERY
OWN TRANSLATOR.

MISTER SIN.

FRESH OUT OF EIGHT YEARS
OF MILITARY SERVICE IN
THE COUNTRY'S ARMED FORCES.

LOOKS LIKE WE'RE IN FOR
A GREAT TIME!

34

BUT I DON'T MIND. WE'RE A LITTLE FAMILY NOW
AND THAT'S ALL THAT MATTERS.

COMRADE GUIDE   COMRADE TRANSLATOR   FOREIGN CAPITALIST

SATURDAY, DAY OF REST. TIME TO SLEEP IN.

KNOCK KNOCK

OH!

KNOCK KNOCK

Mmmmmm.

Hello.

BANG

MGGRMMM~~ THANKS FOR THE PRIVACY!

HALF ASLEEP, I GO DOWNSTAIRS FOR A COFFEE.

IT'S ALWAYS A PLEASURE IN THESE COUNTRIES TO PAY $5 FOR A LOUSY CUP OF INSTANT COFFEE.

JEEZUS! THIS MUST BE MONTE CARLO!

35

I ORDER FRENCH TOAST.

OUWAN FRRRANSHE TOAST PLEEZZ.

MY MOTHER USED TO MAKE IT FOR ME WHEN I WAS A KID, WITH LOTS OF BROWN SUGAR ON TOP... MMM.

RENE SIMARD

A SLICE OF BREAD DIPPED IN MILK AND HEATED IN THE MICRO- WAVE. THE KOREAN RECIPE IS NO PAVLOV- IAN TRIGGER FOR HAPPY CHILDHOOD MEMORIES.

I MEET THE TWO FRENCH ENGINEERS WHO ARE ABOUT TO LEAVE.

IN ALL, THEY UNLOADED $500,000 WORTH OF HARDWARE FOR DIGITAL BROADCASTING TO ASIA AND RUSSIA.

I FINISH UNPACKING AND SUDDENLY REMEMBER A HIGHLY ILLEGAL ITEM STOWED AWAY IN MY BAGS.

A LITTLE POCKET RADIO !

AN ITEM I SHOULD HAVE DECLARED (ACCORDING TO THE FORM I HAD TO FILL OUT ON THE PLANE).

I COULDN'T RESIST BRINGING IT. NORTH KOREAN RADIOS ARE ALL LOCKED ONTO OFFICIAL STATIONS. CURIOSITY GOT THE BETTER OF ME.

APPARENTLY, RADIOS ARE SEALED AND CHECKED EVERY 3 MONTHS TO PREVENT TAMPERING.

I SLOWLY TURN THE DIAL, FEELING DELICIOUSLY INSUBORDINATE.

IN HIS BOOK *THE AQUARIUMS OF PYONGYANG*, KANG CHOL-HWAN, A PRISON CAMP SURVIVOR, TELLS HOW HE WAS DENOUNCED BY A FRIEND FOR LISTENING TO FOREIGN RADIO BROADCASTS. TIPPED OFF IN TIME, HE MANAGED TO ESCAPE TO CHINA IN AUGUST 1992.

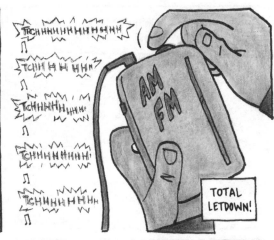

TRCHHHHHHHHHHHH

TCHHHHHHH

TCHHHHHHHH

TCHHHHHHHHH

TCHHHHHHHHH

TOTAL LETDOWN!

HEY! WE'VE GOT NEWCOMERS ON THE FLOOR...

YOU CAN PICK UP A DOZEN FREQUENCIES ON AM AND FM, BUT THEY ALL PLAY THE SAME STATION.

YOU DON'T HAVE TO BE PSYCHIC TO KNOW THEY'RE CHINESE.

THEY LEAVE THE DOOR OPEN, WATCH TELEVISION IN THEIR UNDERWEAR...

... AND YELL TO EACH OTHER FROM ROOM TO ROOM UNTIL LATE INTO THE NIGHT.

YO MAYO CHE FAN!

TSE SUO TSAÏN HAR!

ANOTHER GROUP OF CHINESE LIVES ON THE EIGHTH FLOOR.

BUT THEY WORK HERE, DOWNSTAIRS.

ONLY CHINESE NATIONALS ARE EMPLOYED IN THIS PART OF THE HOTEL, WITH ITS CASINO, SAUNA, RESTAURANT AND DISCO.

THE BENEFIT OF FOREIGNERS IS THEY DON'T SPEAK KOREAN, PREVENTING CONTACT WITH THE LOCALS. WHICH IS HARDLY A THREAT, SINCE THEY CAN'T LEAVE THE ISLAND.

NORTH KOREANS ARE BARRED FROM THIS MINI LAS VEGAS, IMPORTED FROM MACAO, PRESUMABLY TO SHIELD THEM FROM CAPITALIST DECADENCE.

WE TRIED TO SLIP PAST THE DOORMEN BUT FAILED.

I SPEND SOME TIME WITH MISTER GEORGE.

"THOUGHTCRIME WAS NOT A THING THAT COULD BE CONCEALED FOREVER. YOU MIGHT DODGE SUCCESSFULLY FOR A WHILE, EVEN FOR YEARS, BUT SOONER OR LATER THEY WERE BOUND TO GET YOU."

I'VE READ THE BOOK BEFORE, BUT REREADING IT HERE IN THE LAST BASTION OF STALINISM REVEALS THE FULL EXTENT OF ORWELL'S PROPHETIC INSIGHT.

WOW!

ERIC BLAIR AKA GEORGE ORWELL

AT 22, ORWELL BECAME A SERGEANT WITH THE IMPERIAL POLICE IN BURMA. HE RESIGNED 5 YEARS LATER, REJECTING THE OPPRESSIVE IDEOLOGY. DURING THE SPANISH CIVIL WAR, HE JOINED THE REPUBLICAN MILITIA. A NECK WOUND TOOK HIM TO BARCELONA, IN THE GRIPS OF INFIGHTING. IN '39, HE TRIED TO ENLIST, BUT WAS DECLARED UNFIT. HE BEGAN WRITING *1984* IN 1948.* ILL WITH TUBERCULOSIS, HE WENT FROM HOSPITALS TO SANATORIUMS AND DIED SOON AFTER THE PUBLICATION OF HIS BOOK.

1903 - 1950

IT'S THE BOOK THAT COMES TO MIND FOR A STAY IN NORTH KOREA.

BIG BROTHER IS WATCHING YOU.

I WONDER WHAT BOOK A NORTH KOREAN WOULD TAKE ON A TRIP TO FRANCE.

THE HISTORY OF THE COMMUNE?

* THE SAME YEAR KIM IL-SUNG, WITH SOVIET SUPPORT, FOUNDED THE DEMOCRATIC PEOPLE'S REPUBLIC OF KOREA.

I SPEND THE REST OF THE AFTERNOON TAKING NOTES, FLOATING ON THE SONIC GROOVE OF MY BRILLIANT COMPATRIOT PLASTIK-MAN.

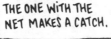

AT SOME POINT, I NOTICE THE STRANGE BEHAVIOR OF THE CAFÉ WAITRESSES.

ONE WAVES A BUTTERFLY NET AS THE OTHER ADVANCES, FLY SWATTERS IN HAND.

THE ONE WITH THE NET MAKES A CATCH.

SHE SEIZES HER PREY.

AFTER TAKING THE FLY FROM THE NET SHE RUTHLESSLY WEDGES IT BETWEEN THE MIRRORED SURFACE OF THE GRAY MARBLE FLOOR AND HER RUBBER-SOLED SHOE, THEN CRUSHES IT WITH GREAT CARE, GRINDING HER HEEL FOR WHAT SEEMS LIKE AN INORDINATELY LONG TIME.

FLY SWATTER GIRL LOOKS TAME BY COMPARISON.

41

OK... WHAT NOW?

THE GOOD THING ABOUT WEEKENDS LIKE THIS IS YOU DON'T MIND GOING BACK TO WORK ON MONDAY.

LET'S GO EXPLORE.

I WANDER THROUGH A SERIES OF NARROW CORRIDORS, ALL PAVED IN GREY MARBLE.

4
2

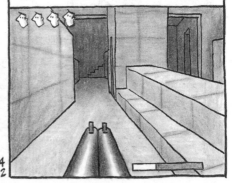

IT'S LIKE YOU'RE IN A VIDEO GAME, TRACKING A MOVING TARGET.

I COME ACROSS A SOUVENIR SHOP, A SNACK BAR, A SAUNA, A ONE-LANE BOWLING ALLEY, A BARBER SHOP, AN UNLIT POOL, A SMALL GROCERY STORE, A BOOKSHOP, AND THEN FIND MYSELF OUTSIDE...

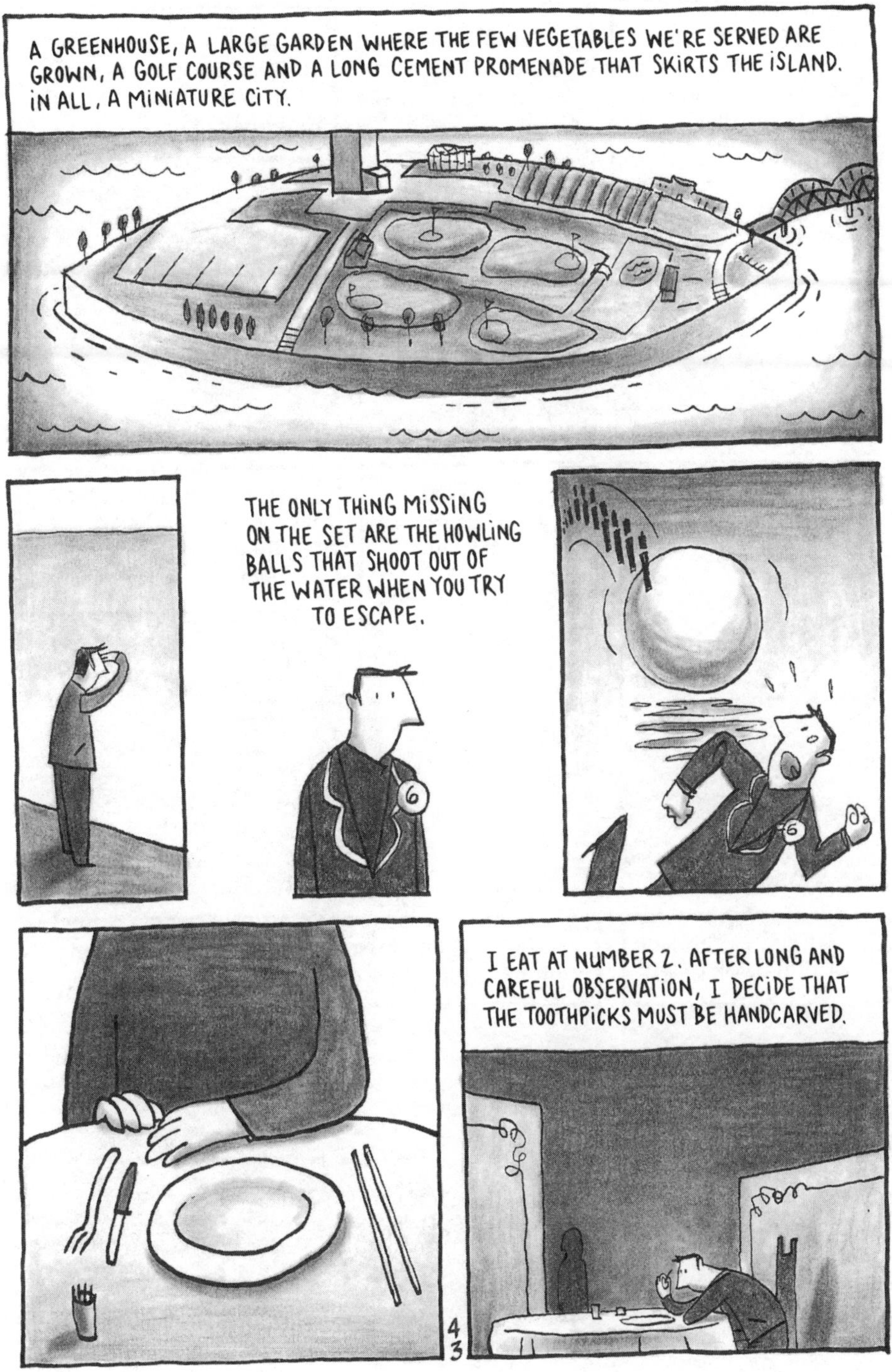
A GREENHOUSE, A LARGE GARDEN WHERE THE FEW VEGETABLES WE'RE SERVED ARE GROWN, A GOLF COURSE AND A LONG CEMENT PROMENADE THAT SKIRTS THE ISLAND. IN ALL, A MINIATURE CITY.
THE ONLY THING MISSING ON THE SET ARE THE HOWLING BALLS THAT SHOOT OUT OF THE WATER WHEN YOU TRY TO ESCAPE.
6
6
I EAT AT NUMBER 2. AFTER LONG AND CAREFUL OBSERVATION, I DECIDE THAT THE TOOTHPICKS MUST BE HANDCARVED.

BEFORE GOING TO BED, I MAKE A POINT OF HANGING THE "DO NOT DISTURB" SIGN ON THE DOOR HANDLE.

IT'S A LOST CAUSE...

HELLO!

AS THOUGH IT'S ABSOLUTELY CRUCIAL, THE CHAMBERMAID COMES AT 7 A.M. SHARP TO BRING MY DAILY WATER RATIONS.

JEEZUS! IT'S EVEN WRITTEN IN KOREAN...

I BRIEFLY IMAGINE A FEW SOLUTIONS TO HELP HER SEE THINGS MY WAY...

THE FANTASY PASSES AND I TRY TO GET BACK TO SLEEP.

44

TWO TRIPS TO CHINA HAVE TAUGHT ME TO HANDLE THIS KIND OF SITUATION WITH DETACHMENT.

mmgrm bitch gmrmm

WHILE BOARDING FOR PYONG-YANG, I MET AN ITALIAN ON HIS WAY TO WORK FOR AN NGO.

HE INVITED ME TO GET IN TOUCH THROUGH THE OFFICES OF THE WFP (THE UNITED NATIONS WORLD FOOD PROGRAM.)

AS WE WAITED, A SERIES OF ACCIDENTS—CAR, SKATEBOARD, BIKE, RODEO— PLAYED IN A LOOP ON THE AIRPORT TV SCREENS.

I GUESS THEY WERE MEANT TO BE FUNNY, BUT BEFORE GETTING ON A FLIGHT TO NORTH KOREA, I WOULD HAVE PREFERRED MISTER BEAN.

SUNDAY MORNING, I MEET MY GUIDE AND INTERPRETER. IT TURNS OUT THEY ALSO LIVE IN THE HOTEL.

THEY RELUCTANTLY AGREE TO TAKE ME TO THE NGO QUARTER.

4
5

LIKE THE BASEMENT OF THE YANGAKKDO, THE ENTIRE NGO AND EMBASSY QUARTER IS OFF-LIMITS TO THEM.

BUT THINGS ARE MORE RELAXED HERE AND THEY CAN ENTER WITH FOREIGNERS.

THERE'S A GUARD AT EVERY CORNER AND IN FRONT OF EVERY BUILDING.

THE PRESENCE OF SOME 100 FOREIGN AID WORKERS IS SEEN AS A SIGN THAT THE COUNTRY IS OPENING UP.

IN FACT, FACED WITH A FAMINE IT COULDN'T CONTAIN, THE REGIME HAD TO OPEN THE DOOR A CRACK TO APPEAL FOR AID IN 1995.

THE CRISIS WAS OFFICIALLY BLAMED ON A SERIES OF UNFORTUNATE NATURAL CATASTROPHES: FLOODS, DROUGHTS...

SINCE THEN, FOOD AID HAS POURED IN, FEEDING UP TO A THIRD OF THE COUNTRY'S POPULATION.

IN THIS HIGHLY STRATIFIED SOCIETY, THE REGIME USES RATIONING TO CONSOLIDATE POWER.

A NATIONAL PUBLIC DISTRIBUTION SYSTEM GIVES CITIZENS PORTIONS BASED ON THEIR LOYALTY AND USEFULNESS TO THE REGIME.

USEFUL POPULATION		USELESS POPULATION	
THE CORE	THE "LUKEWARM"	THE "HOSTILE"	
RICE		250 grams / DAY *	
- PARTY CADRES - ARMY OFFICERS	- SKILLED WORKERS - SOLDIERS, DIPLOMATS (PYONGYANG RESIDENTS)	- CHILDREN OF DISSIDENT PARENTS - POLITICAL PRISONERS (APPROX. 200,000) - LABORERS	AN ADDITIONAL 5 TO 6 MILLION INDIVIDUALS, IGNORED BY THE REGIME, ARE LEFT TO FEND FOR THEMSELVES.

*EQUIVALENT TO HALF THE PORTION DISTRIBUTED BY THE UN IN REFUGEE CAMPS ELSEWHERE IN THE WORLD

AS A RESULT, SEVERAL NGOS - LIKE OXFAM, DOCTORS OF THE WORLD AND DOCTORS WITHOUT BORDERS - LEFT AFTER A FEW YEARS, CONCLUDING THAT AID WAS BEING DIVERTED AWAY FROM THE PEOPLE.

... LEAVING BEHIND HUMANITARIAN INITIATIVES THAT ESSENTIALLY PROP UP THE EXISTING REGIME.

IN ANY CASE, THE DEAR LEADER'S INTENTIONS HAVE BEEN PUBLIC KNOWLEDGE SINCE 96.

ONLY 30% OF THE POPULATION WOULD NEED TO SURVIVE TO RECONSTRUCT A VICTORIOUS SOCIETY.

47

LATER I PLAY GOLF WITH RICHARD AND WE TRY THE CHINESE RESTAURANT IN THE BASEMENT, WHICH LIVES UP TO ITS REPUTATION.

NOBODY'S THERE.

OOOOH NICE!

MMMMM DELICIOUS

AFTER A FEW ROUNDS OF POOL, IT'S TIME TO GO. BUT THERE'S A PROBLEM...

ALL RIGHT... WHERE'S MY GUIDE?

BECAUSE (A) HIS GUIDE, UNABLE TO JOIN US, SIMPLY LEFT, (B) FOREIGNERS CAN'T TAKE TAXIS WITHOUT A GUIDE, AND (C) NORTH KOREANS CAN'T TAKE TAXIS AFTER 10 P.M. UNLESS ACCOMPANIED BY A FOREIGNER.

MY GUIDE

AND SO I ACCOMPANY MY GUIDE WHO ACCOMPANIES RICHARD THROUGH A CITY LIT ONLY BY THE HEADLIGHTS OF CARS AND MONUMENTS TO THE GLORY OF THE GREAT LEADER.

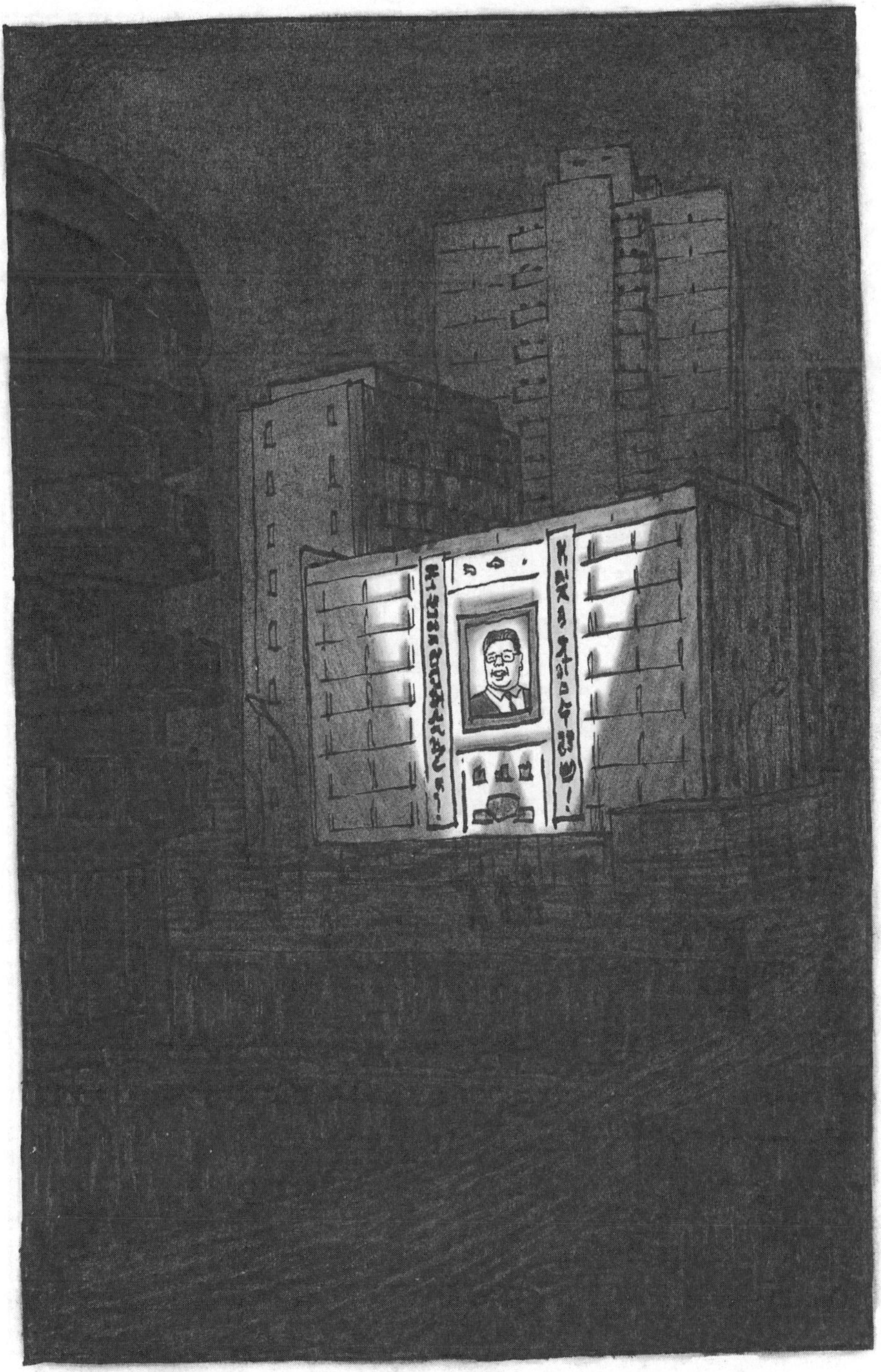

OH NO, THE CHILDREN ARE LOST IN THE SNOW-STORM!
HOW TERRIBLE! THEY'LL FREEZE TO DEATH!
SCENE (201): IMPORTANT! When the father finds out the children are lost, he should not be smiling.
NO
YES
WHY ME...
WHILE I WRITE THE RETAKE NOTES, MY TRANSLATOR MAKES HIMSELF USEFUL ELSEWHERE. THAT DOESN'T PREVENT ONE OF THE TWO ANIMATION DIRECTORS FROM COMING TO CHAT.
INITIALLY, I TRIED TO CONVEY THAT I DON'T UNDERSTAND KOREAN (ESPECIALLY NORTH KOREAN) BUT HE JUST KEPT COMING BACK FOR MORE.
...EVEN AFTER I CUT OUT THE CHARADES.
SO, WASTING TIME?
YESSIR, AS YOU CAN SEE, I'M BUSY!
I GET THE SAME WAY, BUT THE FEELING PASSES.
OF COURSE, SURE, NO DOUBT.
DON'T WORRY – THINGS ALWAYS WORK OUT IN THE END!
WELL, I WON'T FALL FOR IT AGAIN.
OK THEN, SEE YOU.
WOW. IT'S CRAZY HOW MUCH YOU CAN SAY WITH A SMILE AND A WAVE OR TWO.

LATER THAT DAY, A STRONG WIND PICKS UP.

FROM THE 7TH FLOOR, I SEE PASSERS-BY RUN FOR SHELTER.

A GROUP OF PEOPLE GATHERS BY THE ENTRANCE TO THE STUDIO.

SUDDENLY, A STACK OF PAPERS RISES UP AND FLIES IN ALL DIRECTIONS...

LOOK AT THAT...

51

THERE ARE PAPERS EVERY-
WHERE: ON THE CARS, ON THE
SIDEWALKS, NEXT DOOR ...

PEOPLE ARE SNATCHING
THEM OUT OF THE AIR AND
OFF THE GROUND.

AND JUST WHEN THINGS
BEGIN TO SETTLE DOWN...

POOF! IT STARTS
ALL OVER AGAIN!

A RAINSQUALL HITS
AND THE WIND
DOUBLES IN STRENGTH!

THE PAPERS
ALMOST MAKE IT
UP TO MY FLOOR.

HA HA HA
HA HA HA!

HEY!
THOSE ARE
ANIMATION
DRAWINGS!

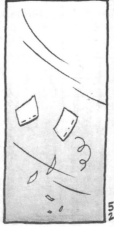

SHHEEEIT!
THEY BETTER
NOT BE
FROM OUR
PRODUCTION
...

5
2

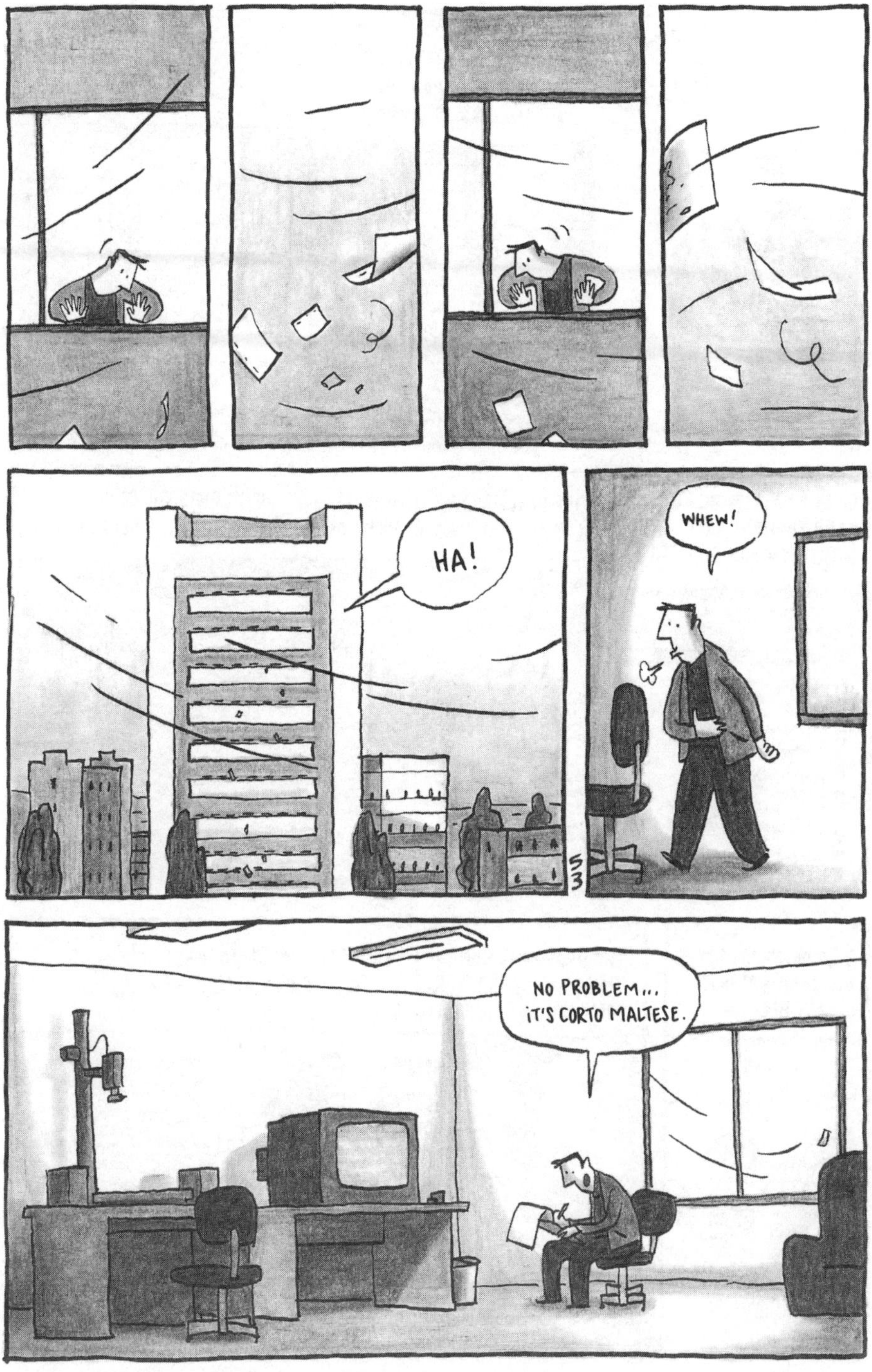
HA!
WHEW!
NO PROBLEM...
IT'S CORTO MALTESE.

ON EVERY FLOOR, THERE'S A HAND-PAINTED CHART FILLED WITH PRODUCTION STATISTICS.

THE HALLWAY'S WEST WINDOW LOOKS DOWN ONTO THE COURTYARD, WHERE AN EXHIBIT OF WORK BY YOUNG ANIMATORS IS BEING HELD.

I GO DOWN TO LOOK, MY TRANSLATOR AT MY HEELS.

THE DRAWINGS HANG IN GROUPS, FROM MOST TO LEAST DESERVING. THERE'S A CHART HERE, TOO, BUT I CAN'T DECIPHER IT. MY COMPANION CAN'T EITHER.

IT'S ALL STANDARD FARE, WITH A FEW SAMPLES OF "TRIUMPHANT SOCIALISM".

BROAD CHEST, SQUARE JAW.

ONLY ONE DRAWING STANDS OUT FOR ITS PERSONAL STYLE, BUT IT'S IN THE BOTTOM ROWS.

FROM THE EAST WINDOW, YOU SEE THE STREET AND PART OF THE ADJACENT BUILDING'S ROOFTOP GARDEN.

IT USED TO BE RISKY TO GROW YOUR OWN FOOD IN THE "PARADISE OF SOCIALISM".

BUT WITH TODAY'S SHORTAGES, THE REGIME LOOKS THE OTHER WAY.

THIS AND THE NGO PRESENCE ARE THE MOST VISIBLE SIGNS OF THE COUNTRY "OPENING UP".

55

I WALK HOME AT NIGHT, PARTLY TO ANNOY THEM, BUT MOSTLY TO CLEAR MY HEAD AFTER A DAY AT WORK.

WHAT, AGAIN?

YUP.

THEY DON'T GET THE CONCEPT. TO THEM, WALKING IS THE MISERABLE FATE OF THE UNPRIVILEGED. DRIVING IN ONE OF THE FEW CARS THAT PLY THE STREETS OF PYONGYANG, ON THE OTHER HAND, IS SUPREME.

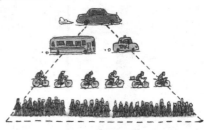

THIS TIME, THEY DON'T TAG ALONG IN THE VAN (THE METHOD WAS TOO OBVIOUSLY RIDICULOUS). INSTEAD, I GET A DESIGNATED COMPANION.

HE LOOKS DELIGHTED.

FINE. LET'S GO.

IT WAS DURING THESE LONG WALKS THAT I WAS ABLE TO TALK MORE FREELY WITH THE ONLY NORTH KOREANS I WAS AUTHORIZED TO ASSOCIATE WITH.

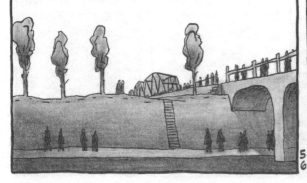

56

AND I HAVE TO SAY THAT DESPITE MY INSIDIOUS QUESTIONS, MY GUIDE AND BOTH MY INTERPRETERS WERE ALWAYS STEADFAST IN THEIR LOYALTY TO THEIR COUNTRY AND BELOVED LEADER.

HUNGARIAN BUSES — VINTAGE 1950's AND GENUINELY MAGNIFICENT — DRIVE AROUND WITH ONE OR MORE STARS ON THEIR SIDES. SIN TELLS ME THAT EACH STAR STANDS FOR 5,000 ACCIDENT-FREE MILES.

GREAT! WELL, FROM NOW ON I WON'T GET ON A BUS WITH LESS THAN 3 STARS...

HEE HEE!

UP AHEAD, WOMEN ARE WHITEWASHING THE STONES THAT DECORATE THE BASE OF THE TREES.

THEY ARE VOLUNTEERS.

HUH? VOLUNTEERS?

YES, VOLUNTEERS.

AH!

I LEARN THAT IN NORTH KOREA YOU HAVE TO BE ON YOUR GUARD FOR DEVIOUS SPIES HATCHING EVIL PLANS TO DESTABILIZE THE SOCIALIST SYSTEM.

THE FIRE THAT BURNED NEXT TO THE STUDIOS 3 WEEKS AGO, FOR EXAMPLE, WAS THE WORK OF ONE SUCH TRAITOR.

REALLY? THERE'S SPIES EVERYWHERE?

YES, YOU CAN'T BE TOO CAREFUL.

WE COME ACROSS SOLDIERS TRAINING TO LOUDSPEAKERS THAT SPEW OUT COMMANDS AND BLARING MUSIC.

58

THOSE ARE STUDENTS PREPARING FOR THE NATIONAL HOLIDAY IN NOVEMBER.

WILL THEY STOP TRAINING AFTER THAT?

NO. THERE'S THE JANUARY CELEBRATION TO PREPARE NEXT, AND THEN THE SPRING FESTIVAL *

BASICALLY, THEY'RE BUSY ALL THE TIME.

THERE'S A LOT TO DO...

* APRIL 15, KIM IL-SUNG'S BIRTHDAY, ALSO CALLED THE DAY OF THE SUN.

WITH A SIX-DAY WORK WEEK, ONE DAY OF "VOLUNTEER" WORK AND PREPARATIONS FOR BIG EVENTS, THE AVERAGE CITIZEN HAS ALMOST NO SPARE TIME.

BODY AND SOUL SERVE THE REGIME.

WHEN I ARRIVED, I SAW A TEAM OF "VOLUNTEERS", HANGING FROM ROPES, PAINT A PRETTY ROYAL BLUE OVER THE RUST ON THE BRIDGE WE CROSSED EVERY DAY.

THREE FOURTHS OF THE WAY ACROSS, THE WORK STOPPED (SHORTAGE OF BLUE?) THE WORKERS NEVER CAME BACK.

TWO WEEKS LATER, THE RUST BEGAN TO SHOW THROUGH THE PAINT.

60

THIS DISPLAY OF EFFICIENCY SEEMED LIKE AN APT ANALOGY FOR THE COUNTRY AND ITS REGIME.

JUST BEFORE THE HOTEL, WE PASS BY A BIG BUILDING.

"PYONGYANG INTERNATIONAL CINEMA"

WHAT? THERE'S A CINEMA NEXT TO THE HOTEL?

THAT IS A CINEMA, YES.

MAYBE WE COULD GO THIS WEEK. A MOVIE WOULD BE A NICE CHANGE...

AS YOU LIKE.

AFTER I INSISTED FOR A FEW DAYS, HE FINALLY ADMITTED THAT THE THEATRE IS USED ONLY ONCE EVERY TWO YEARS FOR THE INTERNATIONAL FESTIVAL OF CINEMA, FEATURING COUNTRIES LIKE SYRIA, LIBYA, IRAN AND IRAQ AND SCREENING THE LATEST NATIONAL PROPAGANDA FILMS TO DESERVING WORKERS.

WE ARRIVE EXHAUSTED. MY LEGS FEEL LIKE JELLY. COMRADE SIN LOOKS RELIEVED TO HAVE PUT THIS WHIM BEHIND HIM.

WASN'T THAT GREAT? FROM NOW ON WE'LL WALK HOME EVERY DAY. HA HA!

I INVITE HIM TO THE CAFÉ FOR A DRINK.

SO, HOW MUCH LONGER TILL REUNIFICATION?

APPARENTLY, IT'S ALL THE AMERICANS' FAULT...

THEY'RE THE ONES BLOCKING THE PEACE PROCESS BEGUN BY THE TWO PRESIDENTS IN 2000.

ACCORDING TO HIM, WITHOUT AMERICA'S IMPOSED PRESENCE IN SOUTH KOREA, THE COUNTRY WOULD HAVE BEEN UNIFIED LONG AGO, LETTING THE SOCIALISTS IN THE SOUTH EMBRACE THEIR BROTHERS IN THE NORTH AND HELP THEM ACHIEVE THE PEOPLE'S PARADISE THEY'VE BRAVELY HELD ONTO SINCE 1948.

NORTH · SOUTH

DREAM ON, PAL!

AFTER THE ASIAN ECONOMIC CRISIS IN 1996, SOUTH KOREANS DON'T INTEND TO SUPPORT A COUNTRY 46 TIMES POORER THAN THEIR OWN! AND AFTER SEEING WHAT WEST GERMANS HAD TO PAY FOR THEIR REUNIFICATION, THEY WON'T BE INVITING YOU OVER ANYTIME SOON! ESPECIALLY GIVEN THAT THE YOUNG (UNLIKE THEIR PARENTS, WHO STILL HAD FAMILY IN THE NORTH) HAVE NO DESIRE TO SACRIFICE MATERIAL COMFORT TO WELCOME A FLOODTIDE OF UNEMPLOYED WORKERS.

CHEERS!

62

THAT'S WHAT I COULD HAVE SAID... BUT I STUCK TO SOMETHING LESS POLEMICAL INSTEAD...

HMM... I SEE,

SINCE W. BUSH'S ELECTION, RELATIONS ARE WORSE THAN EVER AND MILITARY MANEUVERS ALONG THE 38TH PARALLEL ARE NEEDED TO PREPARE FOR IMMINENT ATTACK.

IT'S A CONSTANT FIXATION IN THE PAPERS, ON TV AND IN CONVERSATION.

EVERYWHERE, THE COUNTRY IS GEARING UP.

TO HEAR THEM TALK, THE WAR ENDED LAST WEEK AND IS DUE TO RESUME ANY DAY NOW.

* THE ARMY IS THE PEOPLE, THE PEOPLE ARE THE ARMY.

THE GUIDE SHOWS UP AND SUGGESTS AN EVENING OF POOL AT THE DIPLOMATIC CLUB.

IT'S IN THE FORMER RUMANIAN EMBASSY, NOW FULLY CONVERTED. I'D MENTION CEAUCESCU'S GLORIOUS DEMISE, BUT I WANT TO THINK ABOUT SOMETHING ELSE AND ENJOY THE EVENING.

THE MOMENT WE WALK IN, A FOREIGNER COMES OVER TO SHAKE HANDS...

HOW LONG DO YOU STAY IN PYONGYANG?

JUST TWO MONTHS. AND YOU?

HA HA HA HA HA TWO MONTHS, HA HA HA HA HA HA!

BEFORE RETURNING TO HIS GAME HE SAYS HE'S HERE FOR 5 YEARS WITH 3 TO GO BEFORE HE SEES HIS BELOVED LIBYA AGAIN.

HA HA HA HA HA HA

MISTER GUY, WHAT'S A DINGUS?

I'M NOT SURE. WHERE DID YOU HEAR THAT?

IN A BOOK I WAS GIVEN. IT'S BY SAN ANTONIO.

OH, I SEE. SAN ANTONIO IS TRICKY.

HE'S TOO HARD. I'M GIVING UP. DO YOU HAVE ANYTHING EASIER TO READ?

HOLD ON, I'VE GOT JUST THE THING.

WHAT KIND OF BOOK IS IT?

OH... IT'S SCIENCE FICTION.

THANKS.

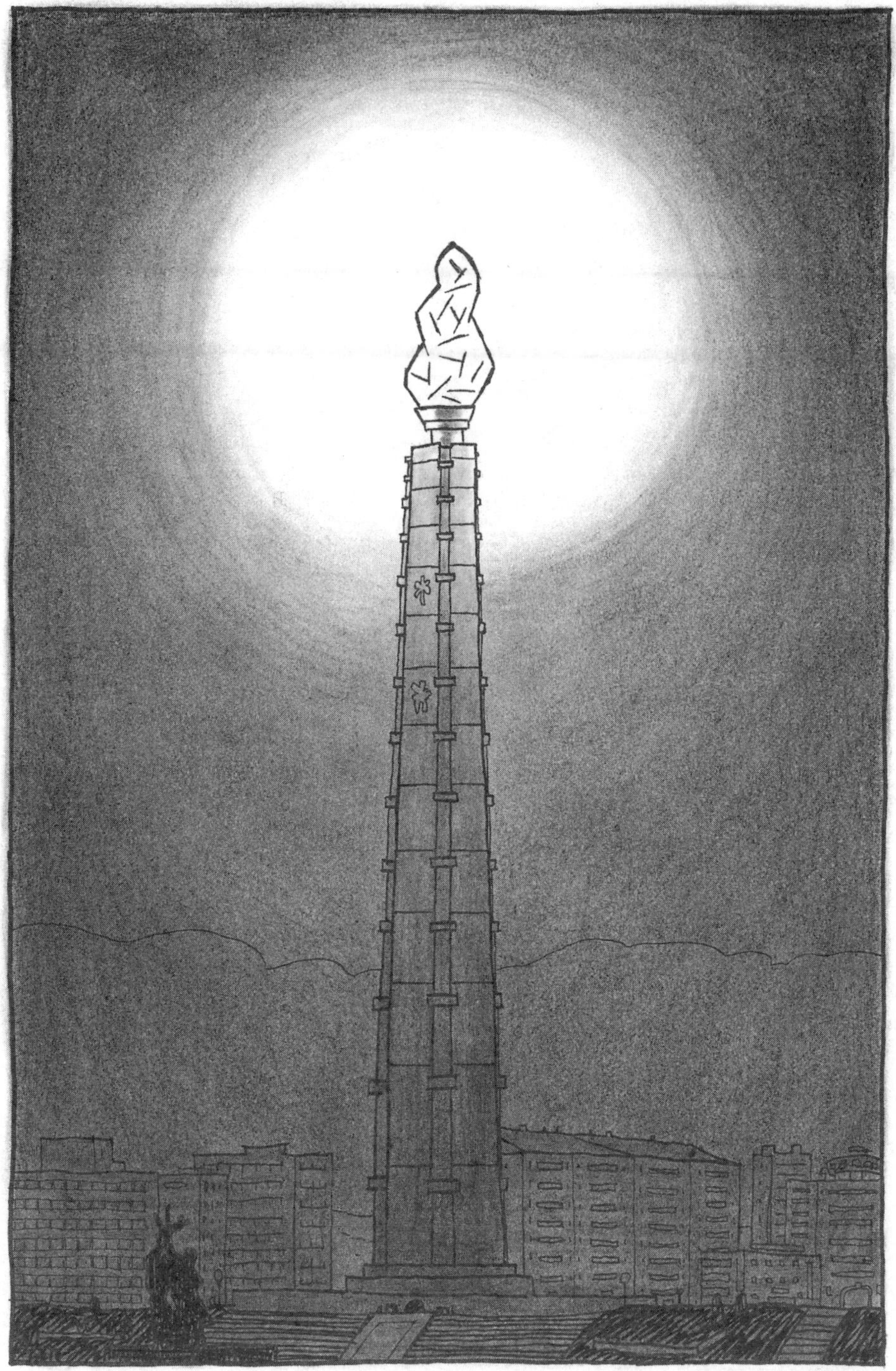

QUIZ

A VILE IMPERIALIST SPY IN THE PAY OF SOUTH KOREA'S PUPPET GOVERNMENT HAS INFILTRATED THIS GROUP OF IRON-WILLED REVOLUTIONARIES.

Which one is the spy?

1 2 3 4 5 6 7

ANSWER: NO. 6, BECAUSE HE'S NOT WEARING HIS OFFICIAL KIM IL-SUNG OR KIM JONG-IL PIN.

IT TOOK ME A MOMENT TO FIGURE IT OUT... AT FIRST, I THOUGHT:

BOY, A LOT OF PEOPLE WEAR THAT PIN.

WHAT HAD ME FOOLED WERE THOSE WHO TAKE OFF THEIR JACKET, AND WITH IT THE PRECIOUS PIN.

IN THE END, I REALIZED THAT EVERYONE, WITHOUT EXCEPTION, WEARS ONE OF THESE OFFICIAL PINS, FEATURING EITHER Ⓐ KIM IL-SUNG Ⓑ KIM JONG-IL OR Ⓒ BOTH KIM JONG-IL AND KIM IL-SUNG.

Ⓐ

Ⓑ

Ⓒ

WOW! THOSE PINS ARE GREAT! WHERE CAN I BUY ONE?

IS THERE A LOT LEFT TO DO ON EPISODE 3?

HOW ABOUT WE GO SEE THE ANIMATORS ON THE 11TH FLOOR? I STILL HAVEN'T MET THEM. IT SEEMS A BIT STRANGE...

YES, FINE. NO PROBLEM.

주사?

위대한 주체사상 만세! 위대한 선군정 치만세! 조선은하나바 위대한점로승좌지협!

선군정지만세! 대위성 돼 한정지 말 와늬대여주 낭주체한족체사삼안세!! 위대한 주체사 상역존나!! 세만사주

CRIPES! IT'S BEEN OVER 10 MINUTES!

IF IT'S SUCH A BIG DEAL, JUST FORGET IT.

SHALL WE?

HOW SPONTANEOUS!

67

WHY DON'T WE TAKE THE STAIRS AND GET SOME EXERCISE?

HEY, WHAT'S THAT BIG CONSTRUCTION SITE ACROSS THE STREET?

THEY'RE BUILDING AN OPERA.

WOW... NO KIDDING, REALLY?

BEFORE GOING INTO THE ANIMATORS' ROOM, WE TAKE OFF OUR SHOES. KOREA HAS CONTRIBUTED A LOT TO JAPANESE CULTURE.

I INTRODUCE MYSELF TO THE TEAM, WHICH I WOULD NEVER MEET AGAIN, AND THANK THEM FOR ALL THE WORK THEY'VE PUT INTO "OUR LITTLE MICKEYS," ALLOWING PARENTS IN OUR CAPITALIST SOCIETY TO SLEEP IN WHILE THEIR KIDS STAY GLUED TO THE TV.

I WALK UP AND DOWN THE ROWS TO INSPECT THE TROOPS.

ANIMATORS USUALLY TACK UP MODEL SHEETS OF THE CHARACTERS THEY'RE WORKING ON.

BUT HERE, INSTEAD OF PHOTO-COPYING THE MATERIAL SENT FROM PARIS, THEY TRACE EVERY-THING BY HAND, IN MULTIPLES.

ANOTHER SUR-PRISE AND IT'S A BIG ONE...

THERE'S A ROW OF RIFLES SET UP ON A RACK IN THE CORNER OF THE ROOM!

IT TURNS OUT THEY'RE MADE OF WOOD.

Hmm

I THINK THE ANIMATORS SOMETIMES TRAIN IN THE MORNING.

GENTLEMEN, IT WAS A PLEASURE.

6
9

...YOU'RE AN HONOUR TO YOUR COUNTRY.

WHAT'S A RAVE?

DAFT PUNK.

IT'S A GATHERING WHERE YOUNG PEOPLE DANCE ALL NIGHT.

A KIND OF EVENT A NORTH KOREAN CAN HARDLY IMAGINE.

SO?

HE SAID HE LIKED IT, BUT I DOUBT IT. THE TECHNICIAN DIDN'T EVEN WANT TO TRY.

HEE HEE HEE HEE HEE

HAVE YOU EVER HEARD OF TECHNO?

NO.

DISCO?

NO.

REGGAE?

NO.

BOB MARLEY?

NO.

REGGAE SOUNDS LIKE THIS...

BOOM CHICK CHICK BOOM CHICK!

GET UP, STAND UP!

CHICK CHICK BOOM CHICK

STAND UP FOR YOUR RIGHTS!

CHICK CHICK BOOM CHICK!

HEE HEE HEE HEE

GET UP, STAND UP!

♫ CHICK CHICK BOOM CHICK ♫

DON'T GIVE UP THE FIGHT!

HEE HEE HEE

NEEDLESS TO SAY, NORTH KOREA ISN'T A REGGAE KIND OF COUNTRY.

I MEET RICHARD AT HIS HOTEL FOR LUNCH. I TELL HIM ABOUT THE DRAWINGS FLYING IN THE WIND.

AND IT STARTS TO RAIN...

HE DOESN'T THINK IT'S FUNNY.

MISTER GUY!

IN THE AFTERNOON, MY GUIDE SUGGESTS A LITTLE SIGHT-SEEING TOUR.

DESTINATION: THE JUCHE TOWER. BUT FIRST A DETOUR TO SEE THEIR ARC DE TRIOMPHE, CELEBRATING KOREA'S DEFEAT OF THE JAPANESE IN 1945. APPARENTLY, HIROSHIMA PLAYED NO ROLE IN PUSHING BACK THE ENEMY.

IT'S 3 METERS HIGHER THAN THE ONE IN PARIS.

SO WHAT? I'M NOT FROM FRANCE.

THE TOWER OF THE JUCHE IDEA WAS DESIGNED BY KIM JUNIOR TO CELEBRATE HIS FATHER'S 70TH BIRTHDAY. MADE OF 25,500 SLABS OF GRANITE, ONE FOR EACH DAY OF PAPA KIM'S LIFE (365×70), IT'S THE TALLEST GRANITE TOWER IN THE WORLD.

IT IS TOPPED BY A FLAME—THE ONE AND ONLY BRIGHT LIGHT IN THE NIGHT SKY OF PYONGYANG.

JUCHE (SELF-RELIANCE) IS THE OFFICIAL IDEOLOGY OF THE REGIME—CONCEIVED, THEY SAY, BY THE ETERNAL PRESIDENT TO MEET THE NEEDS OF THE MASSES AND FILL THE GAPS IN MARXISM-LENINISM AND MAOISM.

AT THE BASE OF THE TOWER, A WALL OF PLAQUES TESTIFIES TO THE ENTHUSIASM OF ADMIRERS WORLDWIDE WHO CONTINUE TO STUDY THE "TRUTH OF ALL TRUTHS".

NEEDLESS TO SAY, EVERY UNIVERSITY WORTH ITS SALT TEACHES THE IDEA OF JUCHE, AND THE NUMBER OF CONVERTS KEEPS GROWING YEAR AFTER YEAR.

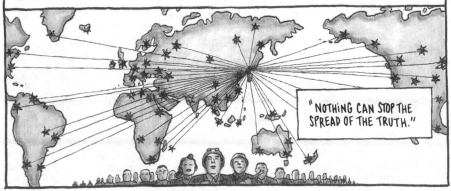

"NOTHING CAN STOP THE SPREAD OF THE TRUTH."

"THE IDEA OF JUCHE, THE SOURCE OF LIFE THAT INVIGORATES THE SPIRIT OF ALL PEOPLE, TRANSCENDING LATITUDE AND LONGITUDE..."

AND TO DIFFERENTIATE AND ISOLATE ITSELF EVEN MORE, NORTH KOREA COUNTS YEARS FROM THE MOMENT THE FATHER OF THE NATION WAS CONCEIVED.

GET SET, GO!

WHICH MEANS THAT INSTEAD OF 2003 IT'S JUCHE 92!

INCREDIBLE! IT'S JUCHE 92, AND PEOPLE ARE STILL CRAZY ENOUGH TO SUPPORT THIS REGIME!

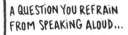 THERE'S A QUESTION THAT HAS TO BE BURNING ON THE LIPS OF ALL FOREIGNERS HERE...

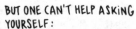 A QUESTION YOU REFRAIN FROM SPEAKING ALOUD...

BUT ONE CAN'T HELP ASKING YOURSELF:

DO THEY REALLY BELIEVE THE BULLSHIT THAT'S BEING FORCED DOWN THEIR THROATS?

FOR THOSE ISOLATED IN THE COUNTRYSIDE, WHERE A SIMPLE TRIP BETWEEN TWO VILLAGES REQUIRES A VISA, THE PROPAGANDA MUST BE CONVINCING.

BUT FOR MY COMPANIONS, IT'S DIFFERENT...

BECAUSE THEY ARE AMONG THE PRIVILEGED FEW WHO ARE ABLE TO LEAVE THE COUNTRY.
EVERY ANIMATION CONTRACT IS AN OPPORTUNITY FOR SOME OF THEM TO GET THEMSELVES INVITED ABROAD TO "START THE PROJECT."
IN FACT, THOSE WHO VISIT PARIS OR ROME ARE NOT NECESSARILY THE ONES WHO WIND UP WORKING ON THE PRODUCTION.

AND ONLY MARRIED MEN WITH CHILDREN ARE AUTHORIZED TO TRAVEL.

IF THEY'RE NOT FOOLED, THEY NEVER LET ON.

AND HOW ABOUT PARIS-THE EIFFEL TOWER, THE BISTROS, THE PRETTY GIRLS?

IT'S FULL OF BEGGARS AND IT ISN'T VERY CLEAN.

IN FACT, THEY LIVE IN A STATE OF CONSTANT PARADOX WHERE TRUTH IS ANYTHING BUT CONSTANT.

IT'S LIKE THEIR PERMANENT FEAR OF LANDING IN ONE OF THE RE-EDUCATION CAMPS.

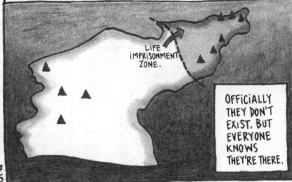

LIFE IMPRISONMENT ZONE.

OFFICIALLY THEY DON'T EXIST. BUT EVERYONE KNOWS THEY'RE THERE.

AND A SWORD OF DAMOCLES HANGS OVER EVERY HEAD, WAITING FOR ONE FALSE MOVE.

STRIKING BOTH THE "GUILTY" AND THEIR ENTIRE FAMILIES.

AT A CERTAIN LEVEL OF OPPRESSION, TRUTH HARDLY MATTERS, BECAUSE THE GREATER THE LIE, THE GREATER THE SHOW OF POWER.

AND THE GREATER THE TERROR FOR ALL.

A MUTE, HIDDEN TERROR.

GOODBYE KIDS!

HM... THE GRANDFATHER'S HAND ISN'T WORKING TOO WELL...

I CHECK RETAKES OF THE RETAKES WITH ONE OF THE DIRECTORS.

HE LOOKS LIKE HE'S WASHING A WINDOW.

OR LIKE HE'S TRYING TO SCRATCH HIS HEAD WITH HIS ARM IN A CAST. HA HA!

NO, I KNOW! HE'S GIVING A SALUTE WHILE GETTING AN ELECTRIC SHOCK!... HA HA HA HA!

YES, HA HA HA! THAT'S EXACTLY IT, AN ELECTRIC SHOCK! DZZT! DZZT!

HA HA HA HA! DZZZT! BYE KIDS! DZZT! DZZT!

MY TRANSLATOR STEPS OUT BRIEFLY, GIVING MY FAVORITE DIRECTOR AN OPPORTUNITY TO BARGE IN.

SO, WHAT'S UP TODAY?

THE PRICE OF RICE? HA HA! PRETTY FUNNY, HUH?

TO CHANGE THE TOPIC, I OFFER HIM A PACK OF FRENCH CIGARETTES I WAS TOLD TO BRING AS EXOTIC GIFTS.

THEY'RE GITANES, NO FILTER.

THAT'LL KEEP YOU FROM LIVING PAST 61.

RIGHT... LIKE GAINSBOURG.

BAD IDEA: BY WAY OF THANKS, HE STAYS GLUED TO THE SPOT, AND AS HE TRIES HIS FIRST CIGARETTE...

HE BLOWS ALL THE SMOKE IN MY DIRECTION.

GLAD YOU LIKE IT.

78

JEEZUS... WHAT IS THAT ATROCIOUS NOISE?

IT'S STARTING TO GET ON MY NERVES...

IT'S THE PROPAGANDA TRUCK ENCOURAGING THE WORKERS AT THE OPERA.

REALLY? DAMN! I CAN'T SEE A THING. THE FENCE IS IN THE WAY...

I HAVE TO GO PEE...

OH MAN, I'VE GOTTA SEE THIS!

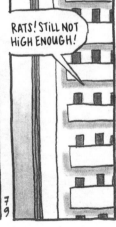

RATS! STILL NOT HIGH ENOUGH!

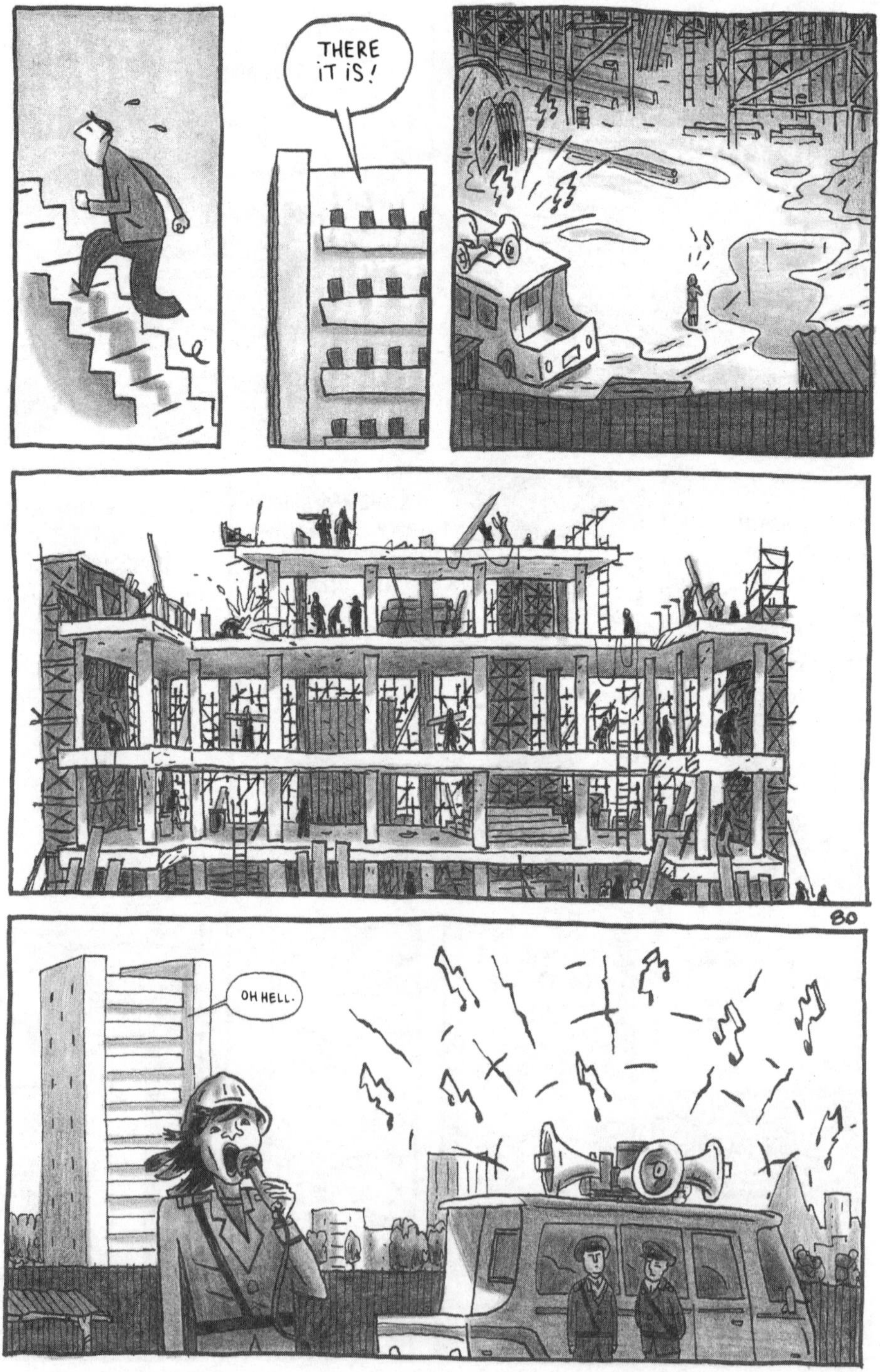
THERE IT IS!
OH HELL.

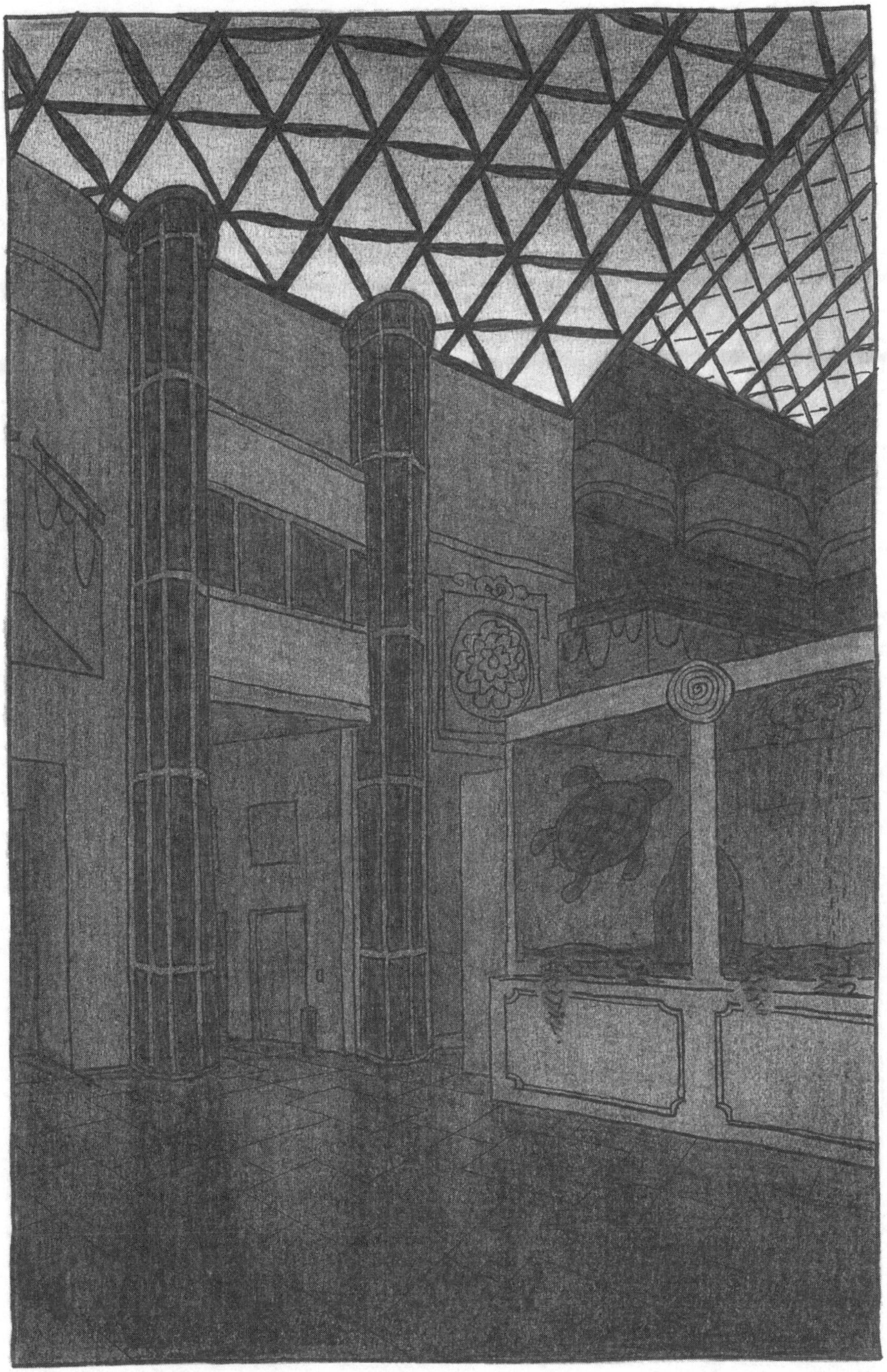

"HOW'S IT GOIN'?"

TODAY'S NEW ARRIVAL IS DAVID, WHO'S JOINING THE PRODUCTION AS BACKGROUND SUPERVISOR. THIS IS HIS SECOND TIME IN NORTH KOREA.

WE GO BACK A LONG WAY, TO WHEN I WAS HIS INSTRUCTOR AT AN ANIMATION WORKSHOP I ORGANIZED ON REUNION ISLAND.

LUCKY FOR HIM, HE HAD THE SENSE TO SWITCH TO COMPUTER-GENERATED BACKGROUNDS...

BECAUSE FRENCH ANIMATION HAS VIRTUALLY DISAPPEARED: IN A DOZEN YEARS, WITH FEW EXCEPTIONS, PRODUCTION HAS RELOCATED TO EASTERN EUROPE AND ASIA.

AND NOW THE CHINESE ARE WORRYING AS THEY WATCH CONTRACTS MIGRATE TO NORTH KOREA.

BECAUSE, LIKE THE MAN SAID, GLOBALIZATION IS GLOBAL.

"IT'S GOIN'!"

I TELL HIM ABOUT THE CHAOTIC END OF THE REUNION ISLAND WORKSHOP, WHEN I GOT A STIFF NECK HOLDING BACK A STUDENT WHO WANTED TO HAVE A GO AT THE SUPERVISOR (NO FAVORITE OF MINE, EITHER...)

AFTER OUR LITTLE TRIP BACK IN TIME, I SUGGEST WE TAKE THE TRADITIONAL WALK TO THE HOTEL.

WHAT? HE WANTS TO WALK, TOO?

HE'S MY FRIEND.

AND THIS IS CAPTAIN SIN, MY GROOM...

WHAT? I'M NOT A CAPTAIN!

DOESN'T MATTER. IT SOUNDS GOOD.

DAVID STAYED SOMEWHERE ELSE DURING HIS LAST TRIP, FIVE YEARS AGO. I GIVE HIM THE GRAND TOUR...

THE TURTLE.

RESTAURANT No. 1

MAN, THIS IS FILTHY!

SHIT, IT'S WET, TOO!

YOU'LL GET USED TO IT.

CONSIDER WHAT A SIMPLE WATER BOTTLE CAN SAY ABOUT A COUNTRY...

THEY'VE CUT OFF PART OF THE SIDE LABEL, SO YOU CAN'T TELL IT'S FROM THE TRAITORS DOWN SOUTH.

AND LOOK AT THE EXPIRY DATE UNDERNEATH...

HEY! IT EXPIRES THIS MONTH.

ASSUMING WATER KEEPS FOR AT LEAST A YEAR, THEIR STOCKPILES MUST HAVE OVERFLOWED AT SOME POINT SO NOW THEY'RE SELLING THE SURPLUS TO THE FEW TOURISTS WHO COME THROUGH.

AND THAT APPLIES TO EVERYTHING YOU BUY HERE. IT'S ALL ON THE VERGE OF EXPIRING...

DING

CHINESE.

OH, RIGHT. I WAS JUST THINKING...

...THAT I'VE NEVER SEEN A MINISKIRT HERE.

84

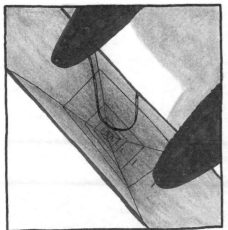

COME SEE... YOU CAN LOOK ALL THE WAY DOWN FROM HERE!

UGH!

HEY! HOW ABOUT WE TRY THE NGO'S TOMORROW? I THINK THEIR PARTIES ARE ON FRIDAYS.

GOOD IDEA.

I TAKE OUT MY NOTEBOOK AND, LIKE EVERY NIGHT, SIT DOWN TO SKETCH THE DAY'S EVENTS ON THE RIGHT-HAND PAGE AND WRITE A FEW NOTES ON THE LEFT.

CHRIST, WHAT THE HELL IS GOING ON UP THERE? WHAT'S THAT NOISE?

IT SOUNDS LIKE SOMETHING CRAWLING...

DRAGGING ITSELF...

A BIT LIKE AN ANIMAL...

A TURTLE, SAY...

THAT'S IT

AND IT'S CRAWLING ...

A TURTLE CRAWLING OVER A DRUM...

VERY SLOWLY ...

STOP!

IF I DON'T STOP THINKING ABOUT THAT SOUND, I'LL NEVER GET TO SLEEP TONIGHT.

OR MAYBE TWO...

TWO FIGHTING TURTLES ...

SLEEP WELL? SO SO! ME TOO.

DID YOU SEE THE MELON?

I TOOK SOME.

IT LOOKS LIKE THERE'LL BE MELON ALL WEEK...

HOW CAN YOU TELL?

EASY—THE LIGHTS ARE ON... AND LIGHTS MEAN FOREIGN DELEGATIONS, AND FOREIGN DELEGATIONS MEAN LIGHT ALL DAY AND FRUIT EVERY MORNING.

LET'S GO, CAPTAIN SIN!

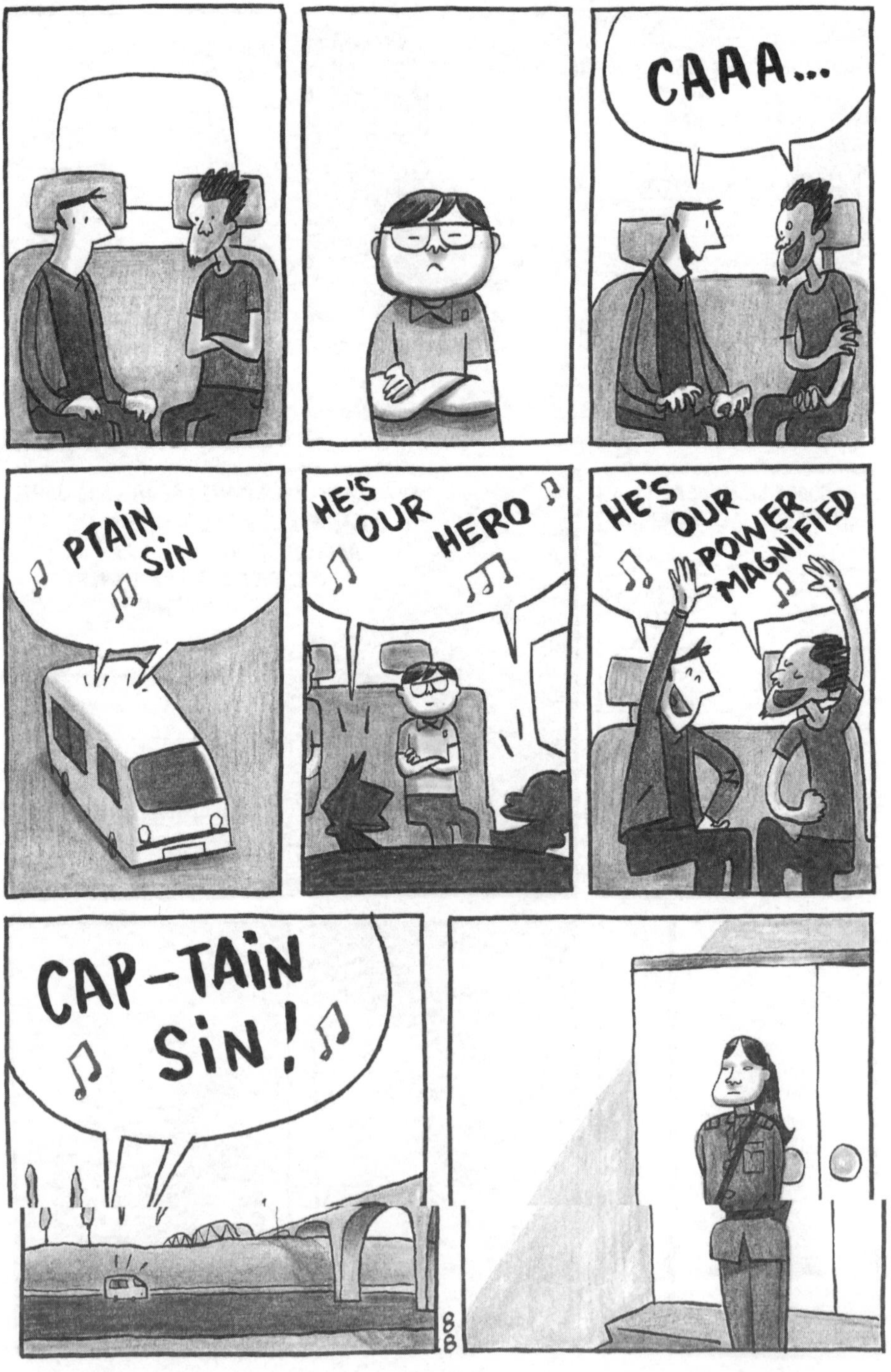
CAAA...
PTAIN SIN
HE'S OUR HERO
HE'S OUR POWER MAGNIFIED
CAP-TAIN SIN!

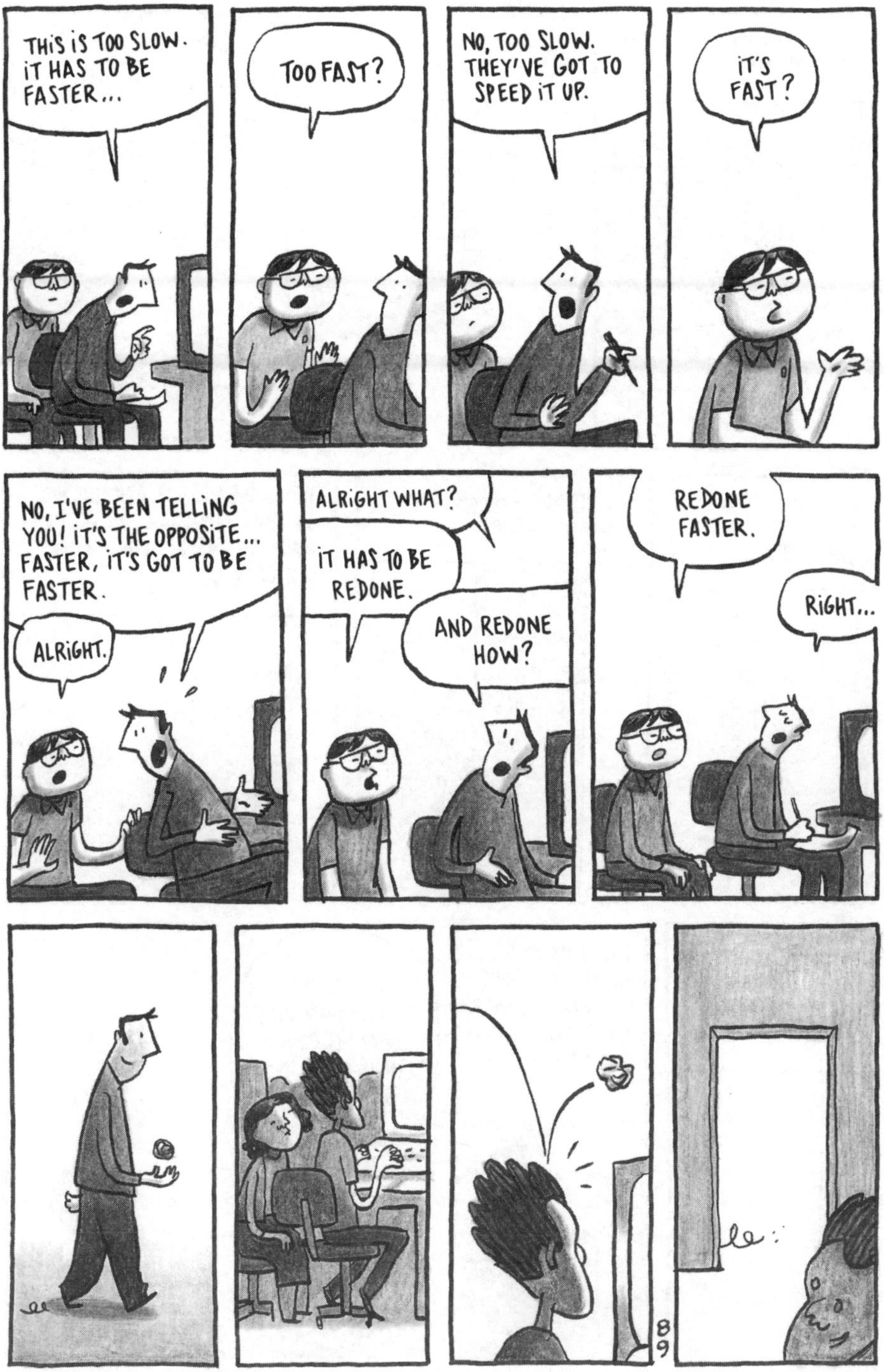
THIS IS TOO SLOW. IT HAS TO BE FASTER...
TOO FAST?
NO, TOO SLOW. THEY'VE GOT TO SPEED IT UP.
IT'S FAST?
NO, I'VE BEEN TELLING YOU! IT'S THE OPPOSITE... FASTER, IT'S GOT TO BE FASTER.
ALRIGHT.
ALRIGHT WHAT?
IT HAS TO BE REDONE.
AND REDONE HOW?
REDONE FASTER.
RIGHT...

IT'S A BEAUTIFUL DAY. I PUT ON SOME MUSIC.

A LITTLE ACID-JAZZ.

I NOTICE MY GUIDE DISCRETELY SHUTTING THE DOOR.

IT'S HOT, SO I REOPEN IT A MOMENT LATER.

HE COMES BACK. I ASK HIM NOT TO SHUT THE DOOR. HE SAYS I'LL HAVE TO TURN DOWN THE MUSIC, WHICH I DO.

HE SHUTS THE DOOR ANYWAY. I'M HOT AND HE'S STARTING TO BUG ME.

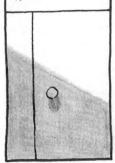

I GET UP AND REOPEN THE DOOR. HE CHARGES BACK AND THAT'S WHEN HE SAYS:

YOU HAVE TO TURN DOWN YOUR JAZZ! IT COULD HAVE A BAD IN-FLUENCE ON THE OTHERS!

THE OTHERS?

WE'VE GOT SOME GREAT ANIMATORS AT THIS STUDIO. THE BEST ONE WAS KIM SON-YOK...

WHO'S HE? IS HE ON ONE OF OUR TEAMS?

NO.

WHAT PRODUCTION IS HE WORKING ON?

HE ISN'T HERE ANY MORE.

HUH? ARE THERE OTHER ANY STUDIOS IN NORTH KOREA?

NO, NONE.

OH, I SEE. HE WENT ABROAD.

NOT AT ALL.

SO WHERE IS THIS SUPER ANIMATOR?

HE DIDN'T JUST DIS-APPEAR, DID HE?

"VAPORIZED" IS WHAT ORWELL CALLS THOSE WHO ARE GONE AND BEST FORGOTTEN.

91

QUIZ

THIS GROUP OF IRON-WILLED REVOLUTIONARIES INCLUDES A VILE ANTI-PARTY ELEMENT CORRUPTED BY THE IMPERIALIST BOURGEOISIE.

Can you find him?

ANSWER: NUMBER 2, BECAUSE HIS BADGE IS SMUDGED AND HE DOESN'T HAVE A HANDKERCHIEF TO CLEAN IT.

WE END THE WEEK ON A HIGH NOTE, WATCHING THE SUN SINK DOWN BEHIND THE CITY.

AT LEAST IT'S NOT POLLUTED.

DRINKS IN THE REVOLVING RESTAURANT WOULD BECOME A FRIDAY NIGHT RITUAL.

HEY, IT'S NOT TURNING TODAY!

TRUE.

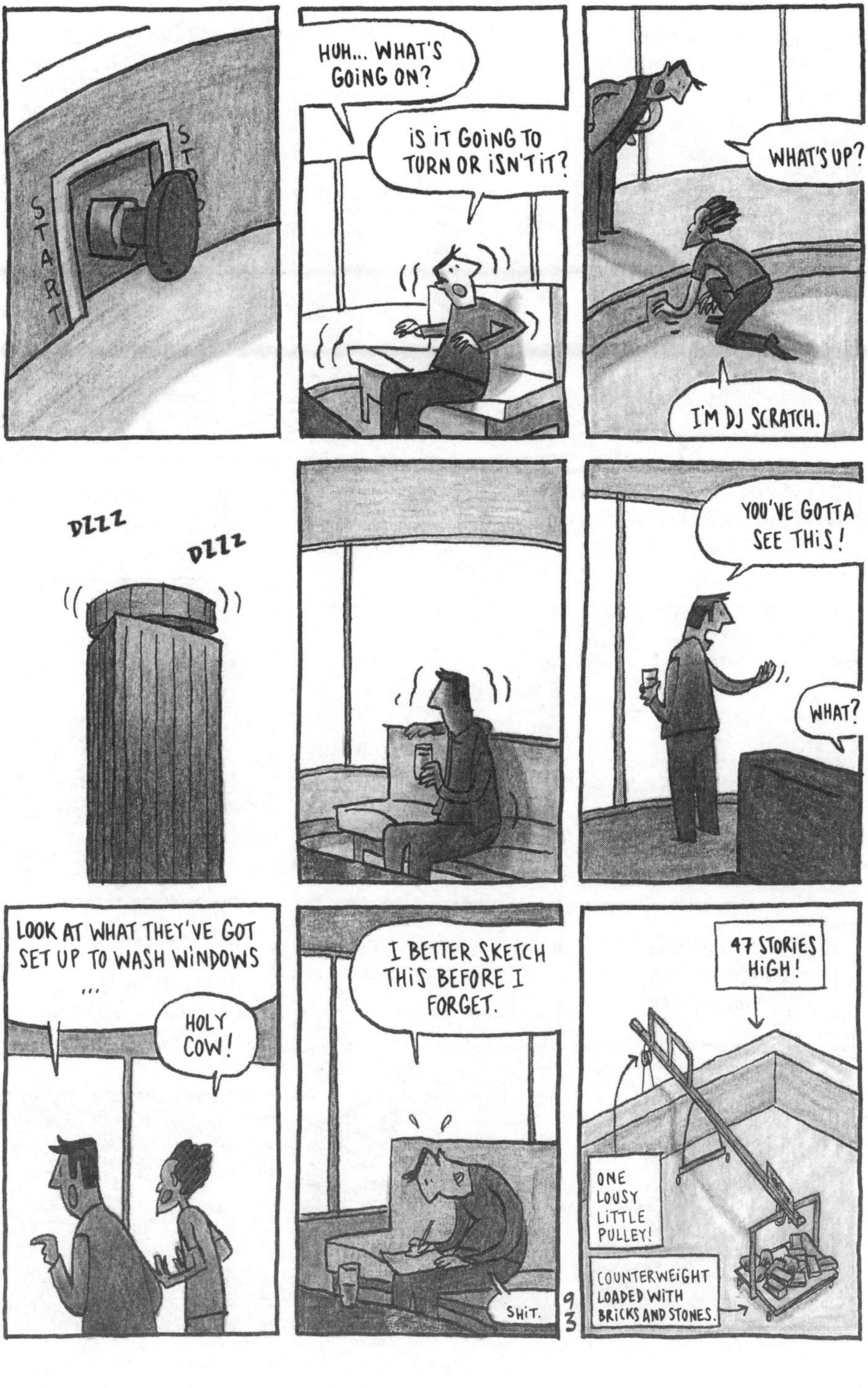
START
STOP
HUH... WHAT'S GOING ON?
IS IT GOING TO TURN OR ISN'T IT?
WHAT'S UP?
I'M DJ SCRATCH.
DZZZ
DZZZ
YOU'VE GOTTA SEE THIS!
WHAT?
LOOK AT WHAT THEY'VE GOT SET UP TO WASH WINDOWS ...
HOLY COW!
I BETTER SKETCH THIS BEFORE I FORGET.
SHIT.
47 STORIES HIGH!
ONE LOUSY LITTLE PULLEY!
COUNTERWEIGHT LOADED WITH BRICKS AND STONES.

WE PICK UP RICHARD AND HEAD OUT TO THE FRIDAY NIGHT PARTY.

THIS TIME, THE PLACE ISN'T EMPTY.

WE LAND IN THE SMALL WORLD OF HUMANITARIAN EXPATS, WITH NGOS AND THE UNITED NATIONS ALL UNDER ONE ROOF.

THEY'RE HAPPY TO SEE NEW FACES AND WE'RE HAPPY TO HAVE DUMPED OUR GUIDES.

A FEW HAVE BEEN IN PYONG-YANG FOR YEARS. I MEET UP WITH THE ITALIAN FROM THE AIRPORT.

GENERALLY SPEAKING THEY'RE SURPRISED TO HEAR WE'RE ANIMATORS.

CARTOONS?

THOSE ABOUT TO LEAVE THE COUNTRY FOR GOOD HAVE TO STAND UP ON THE BAR.

SPEECH! SPEEECH!

THERE ARE PEOPLE OF ALL AGES, MEN, WOMEN...

AND I REALIZE THAT AFTER SPENDING SO MUCH TIME WITH LOCALS IN UNIFORM, I'D ALMOST FORGOTTEN THAT WOMEN COULD HAVE SO MANY CURVES.

A RATHER ODD EAST GERMAN TALKS MY LEG OFF. HE WAS HERE BEFORE THE FALL OF THE SOVIET UNION AND SAYS HE IMPORTED THE SUBWAY TRAINS USED IN PYONGYANG.

I RUN INTO A FEW FRENCH NATIONALS DOING AGRICULTURAL DEVELOPMENT WORK FOR THE ONLY FRENCH NGO IN THE COUNTRY.

I MEET A WOMAN FROM MONGOLIA.

YOU ARE MONGOLIAN? UH... NO.. MONGOL?

LATE THAT NIGHT, WE GET A RIDE FROM ROBERTO, AN ARGENTINIAN WHO SPEAKS MOST EUROPEAN LANGUAGES AND IS AS SOUSED AS WE ARE.

WHICH DOESN'T STOP HIM FROM SPEEDING AS HE ZIGZAGS AROUND THE ZOMBIES OF THE NIGHT.

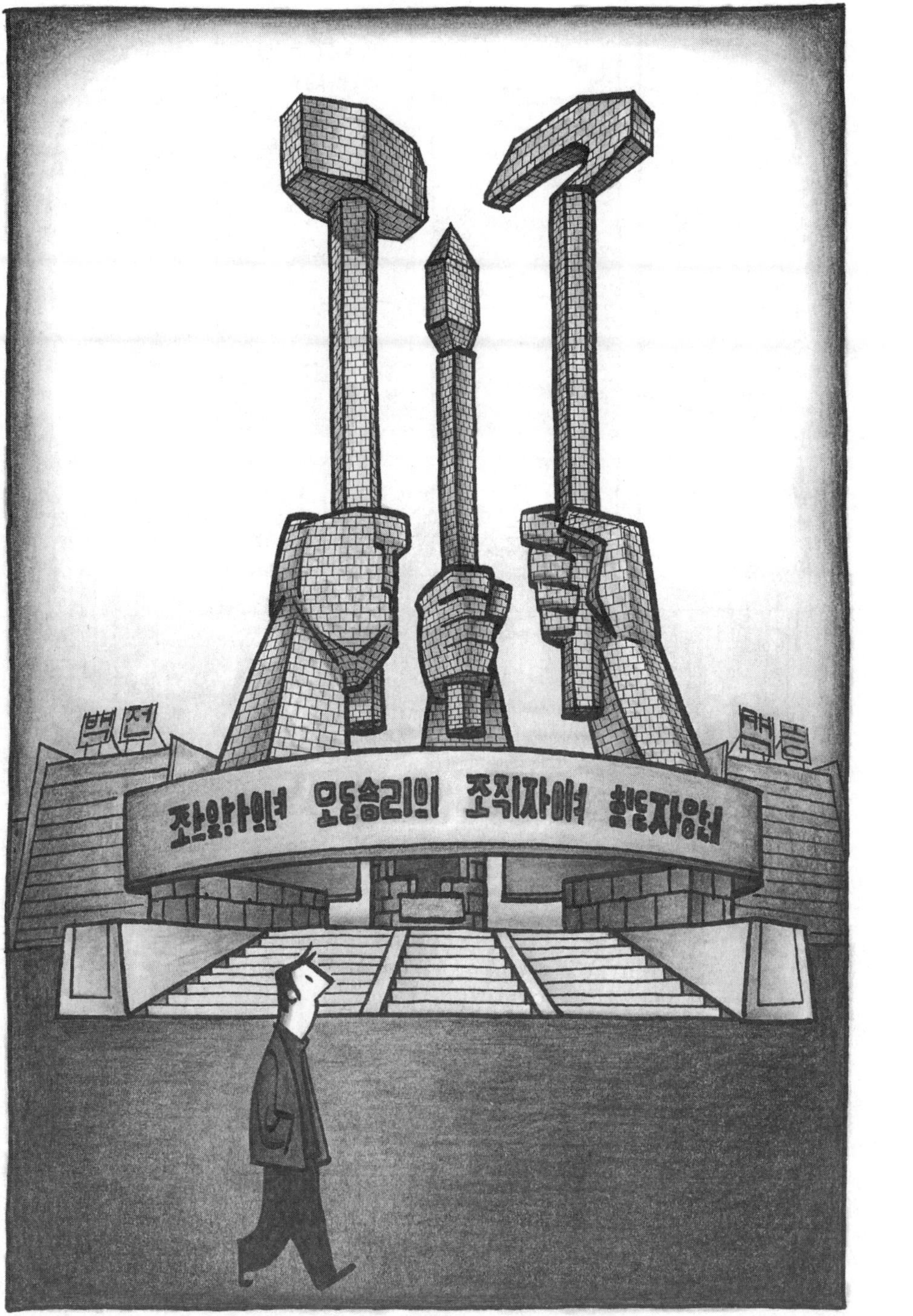
백전

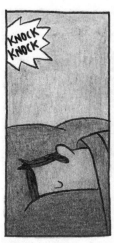

KNOCK
KNOCK

OH NO,
NOT AGAIN.

MISTER GUY, ARE
YOU READY?

I HAD KIND OF FOR-
GOTTEN THAT MY GUIDE
WAS TAKING ME TO
SEE ONE OF THE
HIGHLIGHTS OF NORTH
KOREAN TOURISM:
THE INTERNATIONAL
FRIENDSHIP EXHIBITION.

DAVID, WHO HAD
ALREADY BEEN,
DECIDED TO SLEEP
IN INSTEAD.

RZZZ

TO GET THERE, YOU HAVE TO
LEAVE THE CITY. SOLDIERS
CHECK OUR PASS ON THE
WAY OUT.

FOR THE NEXT TWO HOURS, WE
DRIVE ON AN IMMACULATELY
MAINTAINED FOUR-LANE
HIGHWAY.

I SEE A FEW VILLAGES IN THE DISTANCE, BUT NO
EXITS TO ACCESS THEM.

VOLUNTEERS?

OF COURSE.

EVEN HERE IN THE COUNTRYSIDE, SLOGANS LINE THE RICE PADDIES.

"ADVANCING GLADLY DESPITE THE HARDSHIPS!"

PORTABLE PROPAGANDA.

THE HIGHWAY ENDS AT THE MUSEUM (IN FACT, IT WAS BUILT TO LEAD HERE FROM THE CAPITAL).

DESPITE THE GRANITE FLOORING, WE START THE VISIT BY SLIPPING INTO A PAIR OF ABSOLUTELY RIDICULOUS SHOE GUARDS.

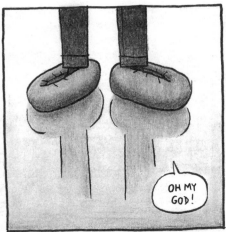

OH MY GOD!

WE CROSS THROUGH A GIGANTIC HALLWAY BATHED IN SOFT MUSIC. I RECOGNIZE THE HYMN TO KIM IL-SUNG.

THE INTERNATIONAL FRIENDSHIP EXHIBITION WAS DUG INTO THE SIDE OF THE MOUNTAIN TO WITHSTAND NUCLEAR ATTACK.

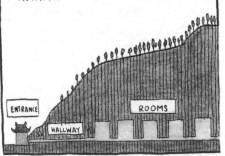

ENTRANCE

HALLWAY

ROOMS

WHICH MEANS THAT IF WAR BREAKS OUT, WE'D BE LEFT WITH A BUNCH OF SWISS, ANYONE PARANOID ENOUGH TO BUILD A BUNKER, COCKROACHES, SCORPIONS AND ALL THE OBJECTS IN THE FRIENDSHIP EXHIBITION.

I'D RATHER BE NUKED...

A GUIDE REELS OUT A STREAM OF EDIFYING STATISTICS.

50,000 SQUARE METERS, 150 ROOMS, 10-METER HIGH CEILINGS, 211,688 GIFTS FROM 174 COUNTRIES.

211688 PRE
174 COU
50 000 SQU

100

EACH GIGANTIC ROOM CONTAINS GIFTS FROM THE FOUR CORNERS OF THE EARTH, OFFERED TO THE "ETERNAL PRESIDENT."

CLICK

HMM... MARBLE WALLS WITH LIGHT SWITCHES IN CHEAP PLASTIC HOUSING.

OUR CONTRITE-LOOKING GUIDE INTERSPERSES THE TOUR WITH COMMENTS FROM PREVIOUS VISITORS...

HE TOLD US: "AFTER SEEING ALL THESE GIFTS FROM AROUND THE WORLD, I DON'T NEED TO TRAVEL ANYMORE."

RIGHT... IT'S SO MUCH EASIER TO STAY HOME.

THERE'S A BIT OF EVERY-
THING: ASHTRAYS, PEDAL
ORGANS, VASES, RIFLES,
PENS, SWORDS, FISHING
RODS, AN ELECTRIC COFFEE
POT, A FLAT SCREEN TV, A
BAYONET, A GOLD MEDAL,
A BRONZE MEDAL, A FRIDGE,
FORKS, STUFFED ANIMALS,
DISHES, AN ALARM
CLOCK, A MACHINE GUN,
ELEPHANT TUSKS, ETC.

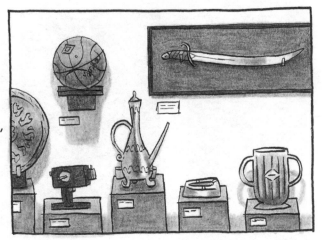

A PHOTOGRAPH IMMORTALI-
ZES A MINER GIVING HIS
PICK TO THE VISITING
GREAT LEADER.

BUT...

?

THE PICK IN THE PICTURE
ISN'T THE SAME AS THE
ONE ON THE WALL.

HMM.

I THINK OF MENTION-
ING IT TO OUR CHARM-
ING GUIDE, BUT
WHY BOTHER IN A
COUNTRY THAT'S
DEVOID OF COMMON
SENSE?

UH...

ACTUALLY
...

FORGET IT...

THE PURPOSE OF THIS GRANDIOSE
DISPLAY IS TO CONVINCE THE MASSES
THAT THE ENTIRE PLANET IS IN AWE
OF THEIR ADORED KIM.

P.S.: THERE'S ALSO
AN ARMORED VE-
HICLE FROM STALIN,
ANOTHER FROM
MAO, THREE FABU-
LOUS RUSSIAN
CARS FROM THE
50s AND ONE OR
TWO SOUTH
KOREAN MODELS,
BUT I'M TOO
LAZY TO DRAW
THEM ALL.

CLICK

AND SO WE MOVE ALONG, FROM ROOM TO ROOM, SPEEDING UP AS WE GO. BY THE END, WE'RE ALMOST RUNNING...

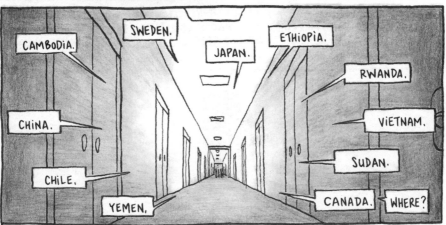

CAMBODIA.

SWEDEN.

JAPAN.

ETHIOPIA.

RWANDA.

CHINA.

VIETNAM.

CHILE.

SUDAN.

YEMEN,

CANADA.

WHERE?

THE LAST SECTION FEATURES PRESS COVERAGE ABOUT THE GREAT LEADER. IT SEEMS LIKE THE ENTIRE PLANET IS GLUED TO HIS EVERY MOVE.

MY TRANSLATOR, WHO IS VISITING THE MUSEUM FOR THE FIRST TIME, IS CLEARLY MOVED.

WHAT A GREAT AND GENEROUS MAN!

LOOK CLOSELY AND YOU SEE CLIPPINGS FROM TOTALLY OBSCURE NEWSPAPERS...

THE METEOR.

I'VE NEVER HEARD OF ANY OF THESE!

AND FULL PAGES BOUGHT FOR A FORTUNE IN PRESTIGIOUS DAILIES.

THE NEW YORK TIMES, DECEMBER 16, 1997.

PROOF THAT YOU CAN BUY ANYTHING, EVEN PROPAGANDA.

LE MONDE

TWO THOUSAND SIX HUNDRED AND SIXTY-EIGHT GIFTS LATER, WE'RE INVITED TO END THE VISIT BY PAYING OUR RESPECTS TO THE FATHER OF THE NATION WHO, AS I'M TOLD AHEAD OF TIME TO AVOID ANY CONFUSION, IS REPRESENTED BY A STUNNINGLY REALISTIC LIFE-SIZE WAX REPLICA.

IMPORTANT! YOU DON'T JUST WALK IN AND OUT OF THE HOLIEST OF HOLY SITES.

MY SHIRT IS STRAIGHTENED.

WE GATHER OUR-SELVES.

SHHHT!

SHHHT!

YEAH, YEAH, I GOT IT!

IT'S AMAZING! THE SOUNDSCAPE, SUBDUED LIGHTING AND SLIGHTLY FORWARD BEND TO THE FIGURE CREATE AN AURA OF SURPRISING REALISM! I FEEL LIKE THE "BELOVED LEADER" IS ABOUT TO TURN MY WAY AND PUT AN END TO THIS UNBEARABLE IMMOBILITY.

OH MAN!

DON'T LAUGH...

BEHIND ME, A DETACHMENT OF SOLDIERS BOWS DOWN, TEARS IN THEIR EYES.

AS AGREED, I BEND OVER ALONG WITH MY HOSTS, BITING MY TONGUE TO KEEP FROM LAUGHING OUT LOUD.

AFTER THANKING OUR GUIDE, WE WIND UP ON THE BALCONY OF THE FIRST PAVILION.

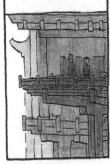

THERE'S A BEVERAGE STAND THAT SERVES COCA COLA TO TOURISTS.

WHICH IS SURPRISING, BECAUSE McDONALD'S, JEANS AND COKE ARE FORBIDDEN IN THIS COUNTRY.

$?

IT'S A GOLDEN OPPORTUNITY, SO I OFFER A ROUND.

NO

THANKS

STRANGELY ENOUGH, DRINKING COKE BECOMES AN ACT OF DEFIANCE. IT ISN'T GLORIOUS, BUT IT'S GOOD ENOUGH.

... ESPECIALLY SINCE I'VE ALWAYS HATED THIS DRINK.

MMM! DELICIOUS.

WHAT ABOUT OUR PICNIC?

WE'RE GOING TO VISIT THE KIM JONG-IL FRIENDSHIP MUSEUM FIRST.

GREAT!

IT WAS PRETTY MUCH THE SAME THING, BUT WITH SMALLER DOORS AND FEWER GIFTS.

106

OUR GUIDE REAPPEARS WITH A GUEST BOOK AND ASKS ME TO WRITE AN ENTRY ABOUT MY VISIT.

"A TRIBUTE FROM THE WORLD TO THE GREATNESS OF KOREA" IS WHAT THE LAST VISITOR WROTE.

Hmpf.

MY DAILY RATION OF HYPOCRISY IS ALL USED UP – I REFUSE TO ADD ANOTHER LAYER OF IDIOCY TO THE BOOK...

I HAVE TO THINK A WHILE TO FIND SOMETHING AUTHENTIC TO SAY ABOUT THIS PILE OF TREASURES.

I've never walked down longer hallways in all my life.

Luckily we were given slippers, or else I would have worn out my shoes.

NEEDLESS TO SAY, I DON'T GET AN OVATION AFTER CAPTAIN SIN TRANSLATES MY ENTRY.

CHEERS!

107

THE PICNIC IS A
REAL FEAST.

AND THE NAP IS
GREAT TOO...

OUR DRIVER IS SITTING BY
THE WATERFALL, SMOKING
A CIGARETTE AND LOST
IN THOUGHT.

CAPTAIN SIN IS PLAYING
IN THE STREAM WITH
A STICK.

MY GUIDE IS LEANING
AGAINST A ROCK, IMMOBILE,
WATCHING RAVENS ON A BRANCH.

THE SOUND OF WATER, THE
SUN HAMMERING DOWN...THINGS
COULDN'T BE MORE RELAXED.

THERE'S NO DRIVER, NO
TRANSLATOR, NO GUIDE. NO
SOLDIER CARRYING OUT A
TASK, A MISSION OR AN
ORDER. JUST MEN LEFT
TO THEIR OWN DEVICES.

108

IT'S UNFORTUNATELY
THE ONLY BREAK OF ITS
KIND DURING MY STAY.

I HEAD OFF TO EXPLORE AND NO ONE FOLLOWS. I TAKE A PATH THAT WINDS ALONG THE MOUNTAINSIDE.

I STOP TO ADMIRE THE VIEW.

A STANDARD LANDSCAPE, LIKE MANY OTHERS IN THE WORLD.

EXCEPT FOR ONE THING...

SPANNING SOME 50 METERS, ENGRAVED AND PAINTED IN RED, A SLOGAN RUNS DOWN THE ROCK FACE, FOREVER SCARRING THE WHOLE SITE.

THEY CAN'T LET YOU BE FOR FIVE MINUTES!

THE NAME OF KIM IL-SUNG IS ENGRAVED IN THE HEARTS OF HIS PEOPLE.

LEAVING THE MUSEUM, WE PASS BY A HOTEL WHERE SOME AMERICANS ARE STAYING. NORMALLY THEY'RE NOT WELCOME IN NORTH KOREA, BUT FOR THE RIGHT PRICE ANYTHING IS POSSIBLE.

I'VE MET TWO OF THEM THIS WEEK.

WHAT! HOW MUCH?

THEY'RE HERE TO DIG UP THE REMAINS OF KOREAN WAR SOLDIERS. FOR EVERY CORPSE FOUND INTACT AND IDENTIFIED, THE U.S. PAYS A PRETTY $ 100,000.

WOW

INCREDIBLY, A FEW MISSING SOLDIERS MAY STILL BE ALIVE. A REFUGEE CLAIMS TO HAVE SEEN SOME IN A RE-EDUCATION CAMP... BUT RECOVERING THOSE WOULD BE A WHOLE DIFFERENT STORY.

UH... A GUY TRIMMING GRASS WITH A SICKLE ALONG THE HIGHWAY — WOULD HE BE VOLUN-TEERING?

THE WAY BACK TAKES FOREVER...

WE CRAWL ALONG THE DESERTED HIGHWAY AT 80 KM/H.

BUT EVEN AT A SNAIL'S PACE WE MANAGE TO OVERTAKE THE PEKING-PYONGYANG!

TO ILLUSTRATE HOW DENSE THE TRAFFIC IS: AT ONE POINT, THE CHAUFFEUR STOPS IN THE LEFT LANE TO GET OUT AND SWITCH SEATS WITH ONE OF MY BUDDIES.

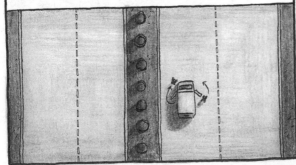

BUT WORST OF ALL IS THE CASSETTE (PROBABLY THE MOST ROCKING MUSIC PRODUCED AROUND HERE) THAT PLAYS IN AN ENDLESS LOOP.

I MANAGE TO MAKE OUT BIMBO JET, COPACABANA AND SANTA LUCIA. ALL INTERPRETED WITH A HUGE STRING SECTION AND TWO-BIT SYNTHESIZERS. IT'S NAUSEATINGLY SWEET.

WHILE I DROWN IN THE BEAUTIFUL WORLD OF CANDY CANDY, I CAN TELL THAT THEY'RE CRUISING THROUGH A REMAKE OF EASY RIDER.

CALIF
HIGHWAY →

WHEW!

I'D PROMISED MYSELF TO LET HIM BRING UP THE SUBJECT, BUT IT'S BEEN ALMOST TWO WEEKS ALREADY.

DING

SO, HOW'D YOU LIKE THE BOOK?

UH... UHM... NOT SO MUCH... UH... I DON'T REALLY LIKE SCIENCE FICTION...

I CAN GIVE IT BACK TO YOU RIGHT AWAY... HERE... THANKS.

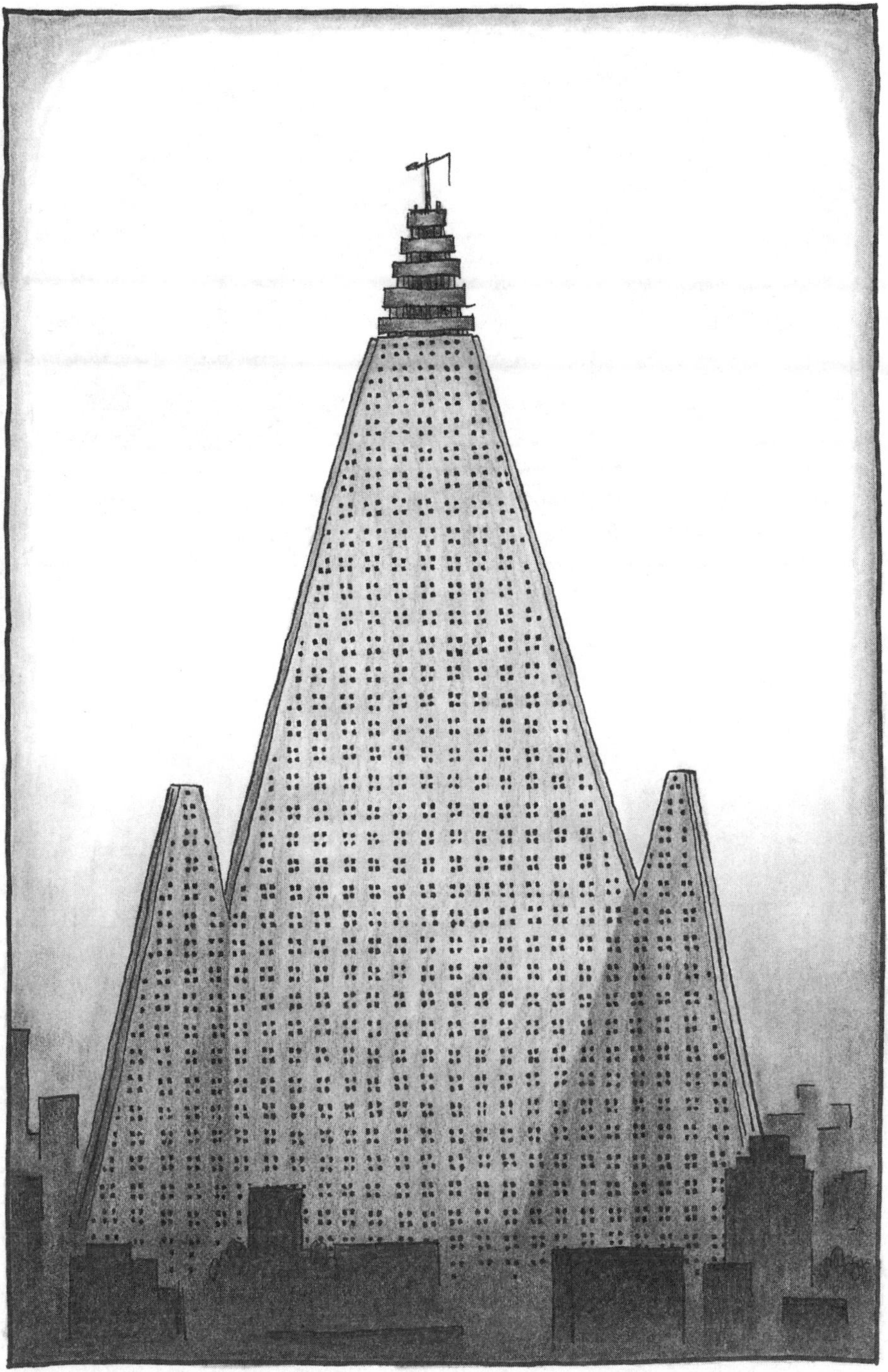

LATELY, I'VE BEGUN RECYCLING THE PAGES OF ONE OF MY STORYBOARDS TO MAKE PAPER AIRPLANES THAT I TOSS FROM MY WINDOW ON THE 15TH FLOOR.

I DON'T KNOW WHY, BUT IT MAKES ME FEEL SATISFIED.

ESPECIALLY WHEN I MAKE IT TO THE RIVER...

C'MON! GO!

I INVITE DAVID TO SHOOT A GAME OF POOL BEFORE SUPPER.

AS USUAL, WE FIND OUR TWO FRIENDS HANGING OUT IN THE LOBBY.

WE FEEL A BIT OBLIGED TO INVITE THEM.

I'M STARTING TO RECOGNIZE A FEW OF THE SONGS THAT PLAY ON THE RADIO.

WHERE TO NOW?

MACAO?

THE FOREIGNERS-ONLY RESTAURANT THAT SHOCKED ME A FEW WEEKS AGO TURNS OUT TO BE REAL HANDY TO SHAKE OUR MULE DRIVERS.

115

MMM... FRESH BROCCOLI.

YOU CAN'T GET IT ANYWHERE ELSE. APPARENTLY THEY FLY IT IN DIRECTLY FROM MACAO.

SATURDAY NIGHTS, EVERYONE WINDS UP AT THE DISCO IN OUR HOTEL—THE ONLY PLACE LIKE IT IN NORTH KOREA.

IT'S BASICALLY LIKE THE NGO FRIDAYS, BUT WITH A YOUNGER CROWD.

AND AFTER JUST A FEW WEEKS HERE, I KNOW MOST OF THE FACES IN THIS EXPAT MICROCOSM.

THE TWO GERMAN WATER IMPORTERS, WHO ARE ALWAYS DRUNK.

AN EXTREMELY FRIENDLY EGYPTIAN WITH PERFUMED HANDS.

SNIFF SNIFF

UGH

JAPANESE STUDENTS WHO ARE LEARNING KOREAN.

THE PRETTY MONGO-
LIAN. UH... WRONG,...
MONGOL.

A MIDDLE-EASTERN
DIPLOMAT WHO HAD
A THING FOR DAVID.

AN AUSTRIAN
WORKING FOR
HANDICAP INTERNATIONAL

A FRENCH WOMAN
WHO MAKES CLOTHES
FOR GALERIES
LAFAYETTE AND C&A.

LOOKS LIKE THE EVENING IS DRAWING TO
A CLOSE! OUR FAVORITE DIPLOMAT HAS
PUT ON HIS CASSETTE OF EASTERN MUSIC
AND IS DOING HIS ZORBA NUMBER.

HE SWINGS HIS ARMS
SYMMETRICALLY AND
NEVER LIFTS HIS FEET OFF
THE GROUND, LIKE A
MAGNETIC TOY.

117

WATCHING HIM, YOU FEEL
THE NOSTALGIA OF A MAN
WHO LOVES HIS CULTURE
BUT IS CONDEMNED TO
ANOTHER FEW YEARS FAR
FROM HOME. FAR FROM
EVERYTHING...

WE END THE NIGHT AT THE CASINO WITH THE U.N. GANG.

WE'RE ALONE EXCEPT FOR A FEW CHINESE, ONE OF WHOM IS BETTING $600 AT ROULETTE.

EVEN THOUGH IT'S A SLOW NIGHT, THE GIRL AT THE WICKET PULLS A LONG FACE AND SIGHS AS SHE TAKES MY MONEY.

WHERE ELSE BUT IN A CHINESE CASINO?

HEY DAVID!

COME SEE! I GOT A JACKPOT! THE MONEY IS POURING OUT!

I SPEND THE ASTRONOMICAL SUM OF 5 DOLLARS AND LOSE IT IN ABOUT AS MANY MINUTES...

AW CRIPES...

WE WALK OUR GUESTS TO THE EXIT.

SEE YOU!

GOOD-BYE!

SO, DID YOU HAVE FUN?

HEY! SHOULDN'T YOU TWO BE IN BED BY NOW?

HOW WAS IT?

AWESOME.

118

SUNDAY, DAY OF THE PEDESTRIAN. THE GREAT LEADER ONCE SAID THAT EVERYONE SHOULD WALK 10,000 STEPS A DAY TO STAY HEALTHY.

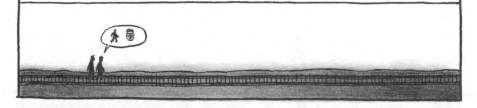

WALKING ALSO HELPS CONTROL POLLUTION IN THE CAPITAL...

IN OTHER WORDS, IT'S NOT A MEASURE TO SAVE ON PRECIOUS FUEL, AS CYNICAL CAPITALISTS LIKE TO BELIEVE.

SO HERE I AM, UNDER A LEADEN SUN, VISITING A BATTLESHIP.

I WASN'T INTERESTED, BUT SINCE HE INSISTED, I GAVE IN.

IT'S THE SEASON FOR TRANS-PLANTING RICE AND ALL CITY DWELLERS ARE "INVITED" TO HELP OUT.

EXCEPT, I ASSUME, THOSE TOO BUSY PUTTING A GOOD FACE ON THE COUNTRY FOR VISITING FOREIGNERS.

HEY! WHAT'S THAT? WHAT'RE THEY DOING?

I DON'T KNOW. I THINK IT'S A GAME.

WHAT KIND OF GAME?

I DON'T KNOW.

WE'RE ALMOST THERE WHEN A GUARD WHISTLES AT US. WE CAN'T VISIT OR EVEN GO ANY CLOSER. WE TURN BACK AND I GET A SUNBURN WHILE MY GUIDE TELLS ME ALL ABOUT THE BOAT.

IN 1968, NORTH KOREAN SOLDIERS CAPTURED AN AMERICAN SPY SHIP IN THE REPUBLIC'S TERRITORIAL WATERS.

SINCE THEN, THEIR GREAT CATCH HAS BEEN ON DISPLAY AS PROOF OF THE SUPERIORITY OF THE PEOPLE'S ARMY AND THE BELLIGERENCE OF THE "NATION'S SWORN ENEMIES".

THEY'RE MORE DISCREET ABOUT A LESS GLORIOUS EVENT THAT OCCURRED A FEW DAYS EARLIER, IN THE SAME MONTH OF 1968.

A COMMANDO OF 31 NORTH KOREANS, ARMED TO THE TEETH, MANAGED TO INFILTRATE SEOUL. THEIR MISSION: BLOW UP THE PRESIDENTIAL PALACE, THE AMERICAN EMBASSY, THE MUNICIPAL PRISON, THE ARMY HEADQUARTERS AND A DETENTION CAMP HOLDING NORTHERN AGENTS. IN THE END, THEY WERE CAUGHT WITHOUT HAVING ACHIEVED ANY OF THEIR OBJECTIVES.

WHEW! ...I DON'T KNOW IF I DID MY 10,000 STEPS, BUT THAT'S ENOUGH!

BESIDES, I'LL BE TAKING A SPIN THROUGH THE CITY IN THE U.N. 4×4 LATER ON...

WITH FRIENDS?

YES.

AAAAAAH! FREEDOM: A COMFORTABLE RIDE AND NO GUIDES IN SIGHT!

AID WORKERS NEED GUIDES AND TRANSLATORS ONLY WHEN THEY LEAVE PYONGYANG TO WORK IN THE FIELD.

THERE ARE VARIOUS LEVELS OF FREEDOM FOR FOREIGNERS. AT THE BOTTOM OF THE LADDER ARE JOURNALISTS WHO COME FOR A STORY.

YOU'RE ASKING A LOT OF QUESTIONS. WOULD YOU HAPPEN TO BE A JOURNALIST?

ME? NO WAY.

MANY AID WORKERS ARE POSTED TO NORTH KOREA FOR MORE THAN A YEAR AND KNOW A LOT ABOUT THE COUNTRY. I ASK A LOAD OF QUESTIONS.

AND WHAT'S THAT? WHAT'RE THEY DOING?

OH THAT. IT'S A SHOOTING GALLERY. THEY PRACTICE ON SILHOUETTES OF AMERICAN AND JAPANESE SOLDIERS.

OOOOH, I SEE!

WE STOP FOR ICE CREAM AT THE KORYO, THE ONLY PLACE IN TOWN THAT HAS ANY.

122

NEARBY IS THE ENTRANCE TO THE AREA RESERVED FOR THE PARTY ELITE. SECURITY IS EVEN HEAVIER THAN IN THE DIPLOMATIC SECTOR: THE GUARDS HERE ARE ARMED. IT'S A REAL CITY WITHIN A CITY - A TERRA INCOGNITA WITH MERCEDES BENZ LIMOUSINES GLIDING IN AND OUT.

WE DRIVE ON AND STOP IN ANOTHER SECTOR TO TAKE A WALK.

WHICH GIVES ME A CHANCE TO APPROACH THE GIGANTIC AND MYSTERIOUS BUILDING THAT LOOMS OVER THE CITY LIKE DRACULA AND HIS CASTLE IN AN OLD HORROR MOVIE.

HOLY COW!...

...IT'S

...MONSTROUS!

ALTHOUGH THE PYRAMID STICKS OUT LIKE A SORE THUMB, IT'S HARDLY VISIBLE TO NORTH KOREANS.

- WHAT'S THAT HUGE THING?
- WHERE?
- THERE... THE BIG TRIANGLE.
- OH, THAT... UH...

FROM CLOSE UP, YOU REALIZE IT'S JUST A CONCRETE SHELL. A CRANE ON THE SUMMIT SUGGESTS THAT IT'S STILL UNDER CONSTRUCTION.

DESIGNED TO HOST PART OF THE 1988 OLYMPIC TRIALS, IT WOULD HAVE BEEN THE TALLEST HOTEL IN ASIA WITH ITS 105 FLOORS, 5 REVOLVING RESTAURANTS AND 3,700 ROOMS. UNDERTAKEN WITH THE HELP OF FRENCH FUNDS AND ENGINEERS, WORK WAS HALTED IN 1989, LEAVING NOTHING BUT A VISIBLY ROTTING CARCASS.

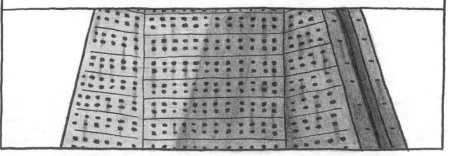

GIVEN THE NUMBER OF TOURISTS JOSTLING TO VISIT THE "PARADISE OF THE PROLETARIAT", YOU WONDER WHY THEY EVEN BOTHERED.

AFTER ALL, WE BARELY FILL HALF OF ONE FLOOR IN OUR 47-STORY-HOTEL.

THE DAY DRAWS TO A CLOSE. I FEEL LIKE I'M FLOATING. ALL THIS FREEDOM HAS GONE TO MY HEAD.

C'MON GO!

SHIT!

SEE THAT?

A TURKISH DELEGATION HAS BEEN HERE ALL WEEK.

THANKS TO THEM, EVEN THE ELECTRIC DOOR IN THE LOBBY IS WORKING.

A SLICE OF MELON?

WHY NOT.

HEY SIN! WHAT'S THAT SONG THAT'S ALWAYS PLAYING IN THE POOL-ROOM?

I DON'T KNOW. THERE'S A FEW.

IT GOES LIKE THIS: ♫ PA-PA-PAM ♫ PA-PA-PA-PA KIM JONG-IL! ♫ PA-PA-PA ... ♫

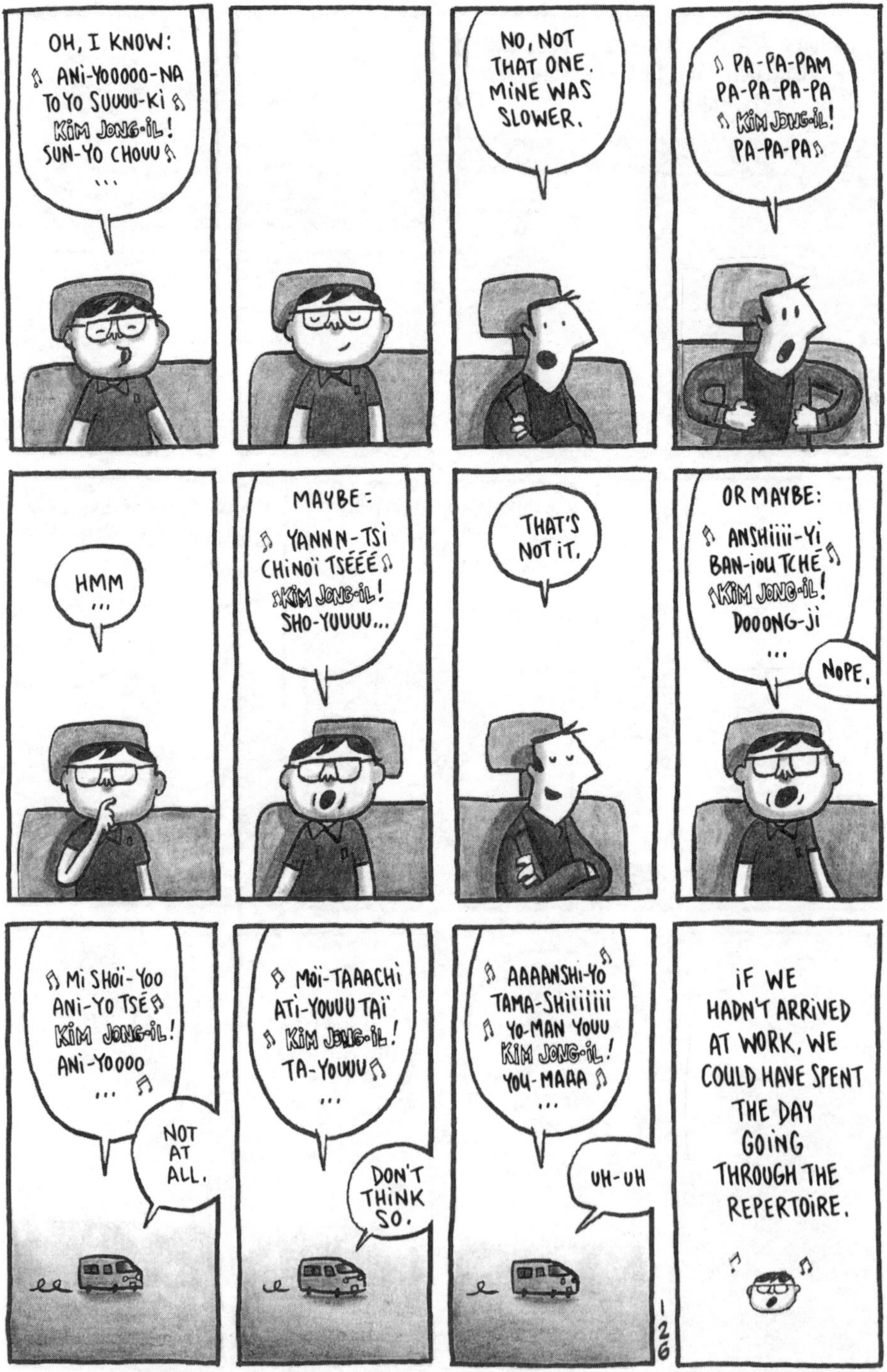
OH, I KNOW:
♫ ANI-YOOOOO-NA TO YO SUUUU-KI ♫ KIM JONG-IL! SUN-YO CHOUU ♫ ...
NO, NOT THAT ONE. MINE WAS SLOWER.
♫ PA-PA-PAM PA-PA-PA-PA ♫ KIM JONG-IL! PA-PA-PA ♫
HMM ...
MAYBE:
♫ YANNN-TSI CHINOÏ TSÉÉÉ ♫ ♫ KIM JONG-IL! SHO-YUUUU...
THAT'S NOT IT.
OR MAYBE:
♫ ANSHIIII-YI BAN-IOU TCHÉ ♫ ♫ KIM JONG-IL! DOOONG-JI ...
NOPE.
♫ MI SHÖI-YOO ANI-YO TSÉ ♫ KIM JONG-IL! ANI-YOOOO ... ♫
NOT AT ALL.
♫ MÖI-TAAACHI ATI-YOUUU TAÏ ♫ KIM JONG-IL! TA-YOUUU ♫ ...
DON'T THINK SO.
♫ AAAANSHI-YO ♫ TAMA-SHIIIIIII ♫ YO-MAN YOUU KIM JONG-IL! YOU-MAAA ♫ ...
UH-UH
IF WE HADN'T ARRIVED AT WORK, WE COULD HAVE SPENT THE DAY GOING THROUGH THE REPERTOIRE.

JEEZUS! WHAT THE HELL IS THIS?

I ASK FOR FASTER AND HE GIVES ME SLOWER.

Cripes!

REDO FASTER!

WHO THE HELL IS RESPONSIBLE FOR THIS CRAP?

I'M GETTING A NEW TRANSLATOR TODAY (WE'LL BE TALKING ENGLISH NOW). DAVID IS INHERITING CAPTAIN SIN.

HELLO!

FINE, THANK YOU!

...?

HE SPENDS HIS FREE TIME READING THE DICTIONARY... THAT CAN'T BE A GOOD SIGN.

HEH HEH!

① OPEN

②

③ SHUT

④

① OPEN

I GO OVER THE WHOLE EPISODE WITH THE DIRECTOR. IT'S A CRASH COURSE IN ANIMATION FUNDAMENTALS.

YOU NEED FOUR FOR ONE BLINK.

AND THE FASTER THE BALL IS MOVING, THE MORE SPACE YOU LEAVE BETWEEN THEM.

1
2
7

NOT AGAIN!

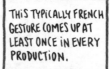

OOH LA LA!

THIS TYPICALLY FRENCH GESTURE COMES UP AT LEAST ONCE IN EVERY PRODUCTION.

OOH LA LA!

AND GETTING IT RIGHT MEANS A WHOLE PILE OF RETAKES EVERY TIME.

OOH LA LA...

UH, NO, TOO FAST. IT LOOKS LIKE HE'S BURNED HIS FINGERS.

SLOW IT DOWN.

NO, NO, THAT'S NOT IT. NOW HE LOOKS LIKE HE'S CUTTING THROUGH A PILE OF BRICKS WITH HIS HAND.

MORE RELAXED.

HUH... WHAT IS THIS? HE LOOKS LIKE HE'S RUBBING HIS BELLY... OR SOMETHING ELSE.

TOO SUGGESTIVE.

THE GESTURE... WHAT DOES IT ACTUALLY MEAN?

128

HM. WELL...

IT MEANS: OOH LA LA...

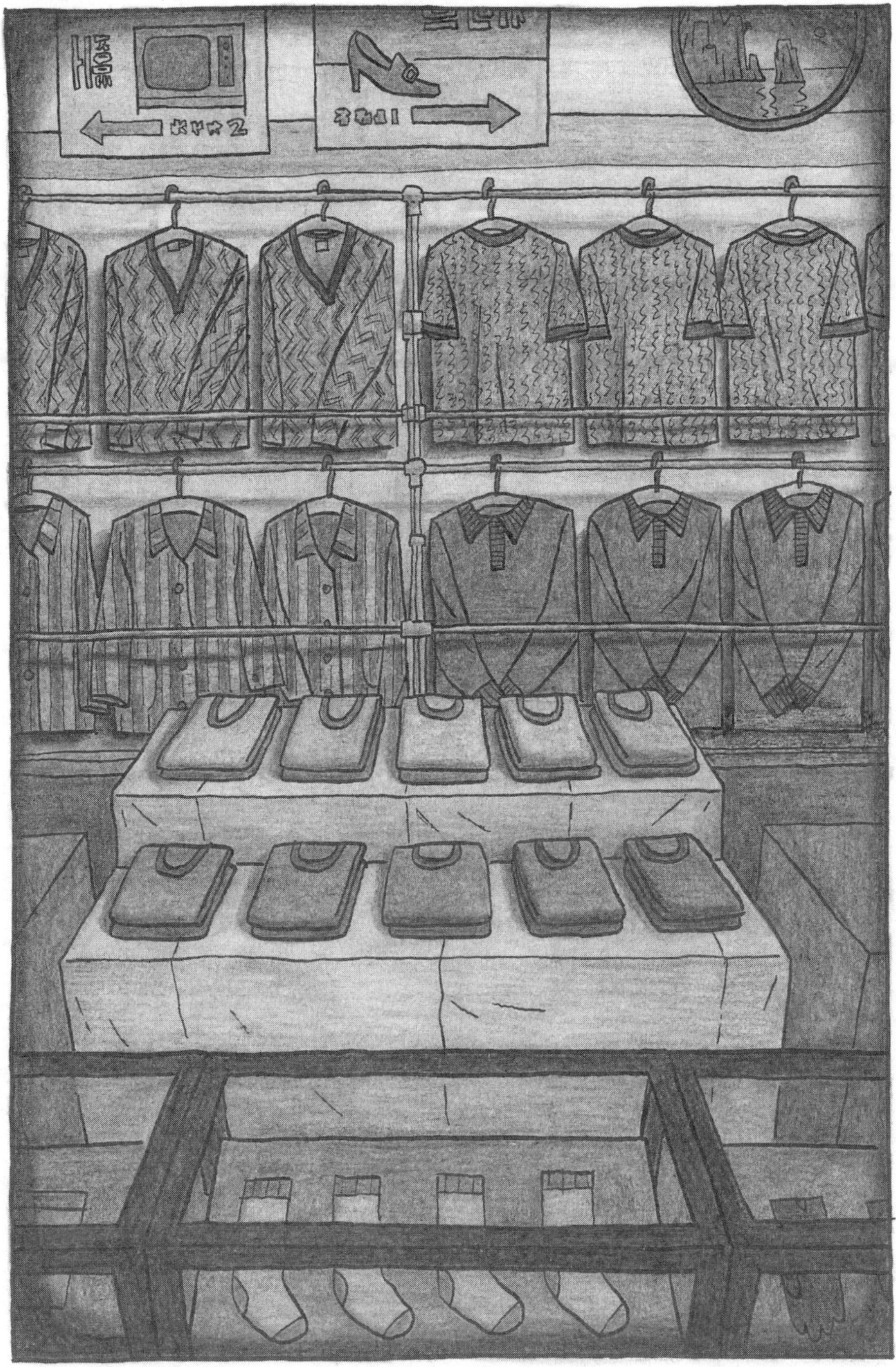

THERE'S A BANNER ON EVERY BUILDING, A PORTRAIT ON EVERY WALL, A PIN ON EVERY CHEST.

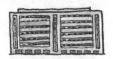

THAT'S A LOT. I SHOULD TRY COUNTING THE NUMBER OF EFFIGIES OF THE DEAR LEADER THAT I COME ACROSS IN A DAY.

LET'S SEE... A SERIES OF PAINTINGS IN THE LOBBY DEPICT ORDERS GIVEN BY GENERAL KIM JONG-IL (WHO IN FACT NEVER SERVED IN THE ARMY).

AS A STUDENT, HE APPARENTLY PUBLISHED NO LESS THAN 1,200 WORKS, INCLUDING A NUMBER OF SPECIALIZED MILITARY TREATISES.

AND IN HIS FIRST GOLF GAME, HE HIT 11 HOLES-IN-ONE.

WHEREVER YOU LOOK, YOU SEE PAINTED OR SCULPTED AVATARS OF THE "PERFECT MIND" IN THE FORM OF A RED FLOWER: THE KIMJONGILIA.

130

THE WALL OF ONE OF THE RESTAURANTS DEPICTS MOUNT PAEKTU, THE HIGHEST PEAK IN KOREA, WHERE THE PRODIGIOUS SON IS SAID TO HAVE BEEN BORN UNDER A DOUBLE RAINBOW AND A SHINING STAR.*

* IN FACT, HE WAS BORN SOMEWHERE IN SIBERIA.

ON THE FAÇADE OF KIM JONG-IL UNIVERSITY, THERE'S A PORTRAIT OF KIM JONG-IL.

ADD TO THAT THE PORTRAITS IN EVERY ROOM, THE BADGES AND THE COMMENTS I HEAR AT WORK.

NOTHING IS IMPOSSIBLE WITH THE GUIDANCE OF KIM JONG-IL...

SURE...

HEY, MAYBE WE COULD GIVE HIM A CALL SO HE CAN TELL US WHAT TO DO ABOUT EPISODE 3?

AND OF COURSE "WE SHALL BE FAITHFUL FROM GENERATION TO GENERATION", OUR LOVELY ASSISTANT'S FAVORITE TUNE.

KIM JONG-IL

CLICK! CENSORED!

SORRY, BUT ALL THIS PROPAGANDA COULD HAVE A BAD INFLUENCE ON ME.

AND LASTLY, ON EVERY FLOOR THERE'S A LITTLE BOOK OF THE DEAR LEADER'S THOUGHTS, HANDWRITTEN AND UPDATED EVERY MONTH.

YUP... I THINK THAT PRETTY MUCH SUMS IT UP.

AFTER MAKING MY LIST, I HAD A DEEPLY TROUBLING EXPERIENCE.

131

WALKING PAST MY ASSISTANT'S DESK...

I COULD HAVE SWORN I SAW KIM JONG-IL'S FACE IN THE MIRROR INSTEAD OF MY OWN.

?!

INTRIGUED, I STEPPED BACK TO DISPEL THE CRAZY NOTION I'D HAD.

TO MY DISMAY, THE HORRIFYING TRUTH STARED BACK AT ME!

NO!

IT WAS ONLY AFTER MY PULSE SETTLED THAT I REALIZED WHAT HAD CAUSED THE ILLUSION.

MIRROR

KIM&KIM

ME

HA HA... WHAT A JOKE!

132

27 28 29 30 31...

I'VE GOTTA GET OUTTA HERE.

SORRY TO SAY, GUYS... BUT YOUR OPERA ISN'T COMING ALONG TOO FAST...

SOMETIMES, WHEN I'M FED UP, I STOP BY THE BACKGROUND DEPARTMENT TO SEE DAVID.

YOU DO THIS.

THIS.

AND THIS.

I'VE NEVER SEEN ANYONE QUICKER ON PHOTOSHOP... IT'S LIKE HE'S ON FAST FORWARD.

THIS.

THIS.

AND WHAT'RE THE MASKS FOR?

THIS.

THIS.

AND THIS.

AH!

HE GETS TO INTERACT WITH A LOT OF PEOPLE.

THERE'S ONE GUY WITH A CAP WHO ALWAYS HANGS OUT AROUND THE STUDIO. I'VE BEEN TOLD HE'S A DIRECTOR, BUT I DOUBT IT.

TO KEEP FROM WEARING OUT THEIR HEMS, THE BOYS WALK AROUND LIKE THIS:

AND WHEN IT'S HOT, THEY ALSO DO THIS:

LOOKING GOOD!

THE GIRLS ARE ON THE CUTTING EDGE OF FASHION TOO...

SKIRTS ARE WORN OVER THE KNEES, AND SHIRTS BUTTONED ALL THE WAY.

IT DOESN'T GET MORE DÉCOLLETÉ THAN THIS.

AND MANY WEAR SOCKS OVER THEIR NYLONS. MMM...

THIS WEEK'S NEW ARRIVAL AT THE SEK IS HENRI.

HE'S A PRODUCER FOR LAFABRIQUE, A STUDIO IN A REMOTE CORNER OF FRANCE WHERE I WORKED AGES AGO.

SO, EVEN THE SMALL FRY ARE COMING TO NORTH KOREA!

IT'S AN ANIMATION WHO'S WHO!

I GET TO HAVE LUNCH AT HIS HOTEL, THE KORYO.

IT'S NO BETTER THAN OURS.

134

THE KORYO IS FAMOUS FOR ITS CAFE, WHERE WEAPONS CONTRACTS ARE NEGOTIATED WITH FOREIGN DELEGATIONS. WEAPONS ARE THE REGIME'S PRIMARY TRADE ASSET.

NICE VIEW!

MY GUIDE IS WAITING AT THE EXIT. I HAD FORGOTTEN OUR EXCURSION TO THE DIPLOMATIC STORE.

THE WEEKLY PILGRIMAGE TO THE ONLY LOCAL SANCTUARY DEDICATED TO CONSUMERISM...

AND AN OPPORTUNITY TO BUY A LITTLE GIFT FOR MY HOSTS.

CLOPES OR GNÔLE?

HELLO BRIDGET... IT'S ME... HURRY OVER! A SHIPMENT OF MANGOES JUST CAME IN!

THE THRILLING LIFE OF A DIPLOMAT'S WIFE.

135

ONE THING THAT STRIKES YOU AFTER WEEKS OF LOOKING AT THE IMMACULATE STREETS OF PYONGYANG IS THE COMPLETE ABSENCE OF HANDICAPPED PEOPLE.

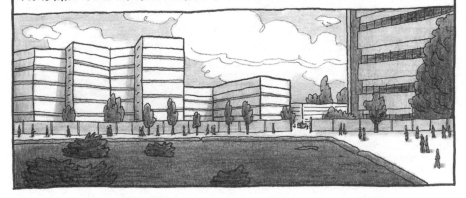

EVEN MORE SURPRISING IS THE ANSWER I GET WHEN I WONDER ALOUD ABOUT THIS...

? ON AVERAGE, 7 TO 10% OF THE POPULATION...

?

THERE ARE NONE... WE'RE A VERY HOMOGENOUS NATION. ALL NORTH KOREANS ARE BORN STRONG, INTELLIGENT AND HEALTHY.

AND FROM THE WAY HE SAYS IT, I THINK HE BELIEVES IT.

1 3 6

TO WHAT EXTENT CAN A MIND BE MANIPULATED? WE'LL PROBABLY GET SOME IDEA WHEN THE COUNTRY EVENTUALLY OPENS UP OR COLLAPSES.

SINCE THE FIRST DAY OF MY STAY, I'VE BEEN ASKING FOR A BIKE TO RIDE AROUND ON.

AND THE BIKE?

BECAUSE THEY FIRST CLAIMED THAT ANYTHING WAS POSSIBLE, I KEEP AT IT.

WHEN? TOMORROW?

OF COURSE I KNOW I'LL NEVER GET ONE, BUT I'D LIKE AN HONEST ANSWER. INSTEAD, IT'S BECOME A KIND OF JOKE.

ANY NEWS ABOUT MY BIKE?

HA HA HA HA

IT'S LIKE THE SERIES OF OUTINGS WE'LL NEVER GO ON...

THE KIM IL-SUNG MEMORIAL WITH ITS SHOESHINE MACHINE.

THE MUSEUM OF FINE ARTS, WHERE 80% OF THE PAINTINGS DEPICT KIM AND KIM.

AND THE DEMILITA-RIZED ZONE...

WHAT ABOUT THE DMZ?

WE'D BETTER WAIT. THE ATMOSPHERE HAS BEEN TENSE SINCE W. BUSH'S ELECTION. IF SOUTHERN SOLDIERS SEE A FOREIGNER ON OUR SIDE, THEY MIGHT FEEL PROVOKED AND SHOOT, AND THAT COULD SPARK CONFLICT.

SPARK CONFLICT...

AND WHAT ELSE...

137

SOME SUGAR WITH THAT?

IN THE AFTERNOONS, RICHARD OFTEN STOPS BY FOR A NESCAFÉ BREAK ON OUR FLOOR. IT'S AN OPPORTUNITY FOR THE REST OF US TO HEAR THE LATEST NEWS, SINCE HE'S THE ONLY ONE WITH CABLE IN HIS HOTEL...

WELL, KIM JONG-IL'S SON, THE ONE WHO LIVES IN SWITZERLAND, GOT CAUGHT ENTERING JAPAN WITH A FALSE PASSPORT... THEY SAY HE WASN'T SPYING. HE JUST WANTED TO VISIT TOKYO DISNEYLAND! HA HA!

AND THE DEAR LEADER IS PLANNING A VISIT TO PUTIN IN HIS ARMORED TRAIN.

YOU FIND OUT MORE ABOUT THE COUNTRY FROM OUTSIDE THAN INSIDE. PEOPLE HERE DON'T EVEN KNOW THEIR DEAR LEADER HAS CHILDREN.

HEY! WHAT IS THAT GUY DOING OUT THERE?

A MAN IS PERCHED IN A TREE ACROSS THE STREET, PICKING FRUIT AND STUFFING IT IN HIS SHIRT.

WHEN I POINT HIM OUT, MY TRANSLATOR BLUSHES AND STAMMERS EXCUSES...

FRUIT SEASON HA HA, VERY GOOD ...

MAYBE HE'S HUNGRY.

MEANWHILE I'VE BEEN PUTTING ON WEIGHT EATING THEIR OIL-DRENCHED MEALS.

Jeez!

SHAME ON ME!

RICE

?

WHAT'S THAT FOR?

PAELLA?

WE FIND OURSELVES IN A HUGE SPORTS FACILITY THAT HOUSES A STADIUM AND 10 GYMS, INCLUDING THE TAEKWONDO HALL BUILT IN 1992.

CAPTAIN SIN HAS COME ALONG.

THE FAÇADE FEATURES A GOLD-PLATED REPRODUCTION OF CALLIGRAPHY BY KIM JONG-IL.

INSIDE, A GUIDE BOMBARDS US WITH STATISTICS ABOUT THE ARCHITECTURE WHILE TAKING US THROUGH ONE HUGE HALL AFTER ANOTHER.

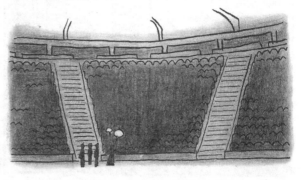

140

BUT I GET THE FEELING THERE WON'T BE A TAEKWONDO DEMONSTRATION: THERE ISN'T A SINGLE ATHLETE IN SIGHT.

WHAT ABOUT THE DEMO? IS IT STILL ON?

UNFORTUNATELY THE ATHLETES HAVE LEFT TO TRAIN IN THE NORTH. IT'S TOO HOT HERE... THEY'LL BE BETTER OFF WHERE IT'S COOLER.

I SEE...

TRAINING IN THE RICE PADDIES, I BET.

BUT IT WASN'T A TOTAL LOSS. WE STOPPED BY ANOTHER SPORTS FACILITY THAT WAS MUCH MORE ENTERTAINING.

FOR THE PRICE OF ONE WON PER BALL, YOU CAN PRACTICE SHARP-SHOOTING WITH OLD RUSSIAN PISTOLS.

GO AHEAD.

I DON'T KNOW.

YOU FIRST!

NEVER HAVING BEEN IN THE MILITARY, I HAVE NO IDEA WHAT THE RIGHT POSITION IS. INSTINCTIVELY, I PLAY IT LIKE CORTO MALTESE.

MY COMRADES HAVE THE ADVANTAGE OF A FEW YEARS OF MILITARY TRAINING.

BUT THAT DOESN'T STOP ME FROM GETTING THE HIGHEST SCORE. HA HA!

YES!

♪♪ CAPTAIN GUY HE'S OUR POWER MAGNIFIED! ♪♪

Imnm
1 3
2 e
3 2

NO!

IT'S FORBIDDEN TO TACK ANYTHING ELSE ONTO A PORTRAIT WALL.

OH!

142

WHY ARE WE WALKING?

DIDN'T THE GUY WHO'S ALL OVER THE WALLS HERE SAY THAT WALKING IS GOOD FOR YOU?

HOW ABOUT WE GO VISIT THE TRAIN STATION?

NO, NO, ABSOLUTELY NOT...

WHY NOT?

NO NO!

ANOTHER TIME?

I KEPT INSISTING FOR A WHOLE WEEK, TO NO AVAIL. THERE WERE A FEW PLACES THEY JUST DIDN'T WANT ME TO SEE, AND I COULDN'T FIGURE OUT WHY. THE PHOTOCOPYING ROOM AT WORK WAS OFF-LIMITS TOO.

ONE SUNDAY, OUT ON MY OWN, I GAVE IN TO TEMPTATION AND VISITED THE MYSTERY STATION ON MY OWN.

HUH!

IT'S A TOTALLY NORMAL TRAIN STATION... WHAT'S THE BIG SECRET?

143

MONDAY MORNING...

SO, YOU WENT TO THE STATION?

IT WOULD BE FASTER BY CAR.

MUCH FASTER.

WHICH IS BETTER, WINDOWS 98 OR WINDOWS 2000?

SINCE KIM JONG-IL DECLARED THE COMPUTER TO BE THE TOOL OF THE FUTURE, YOU CAN EXPRESS INTEREST IN IT WITHOUT SOUNDING LIKE AN ENEMY OF THE REGIME.

STRANGELY ENOUGH, HE ALSO DECLARED BICYCLES TO BE HAZARDOUS FOR WOMEN. THEY ALL RIDE TRICYCLES NOW.

SO MY TRANSLATOR, WHO IS ALLOWED TO RIDE A BIKE, KEEPS ASKING QUESTIONS ABOUT COMPUTERS.

AND WHAT ABOUT HTML?

IF WE HAD INTERNET ACCESS, YOU COULD GIVE IT A TRY.

DO YOU REALIZE THAT THIS IS THE ONLY COUNTRY THAT ISN'T CONNECTED TO THE NET?

OH NO... DON'T SAY THAT!

IT'S TRUE...

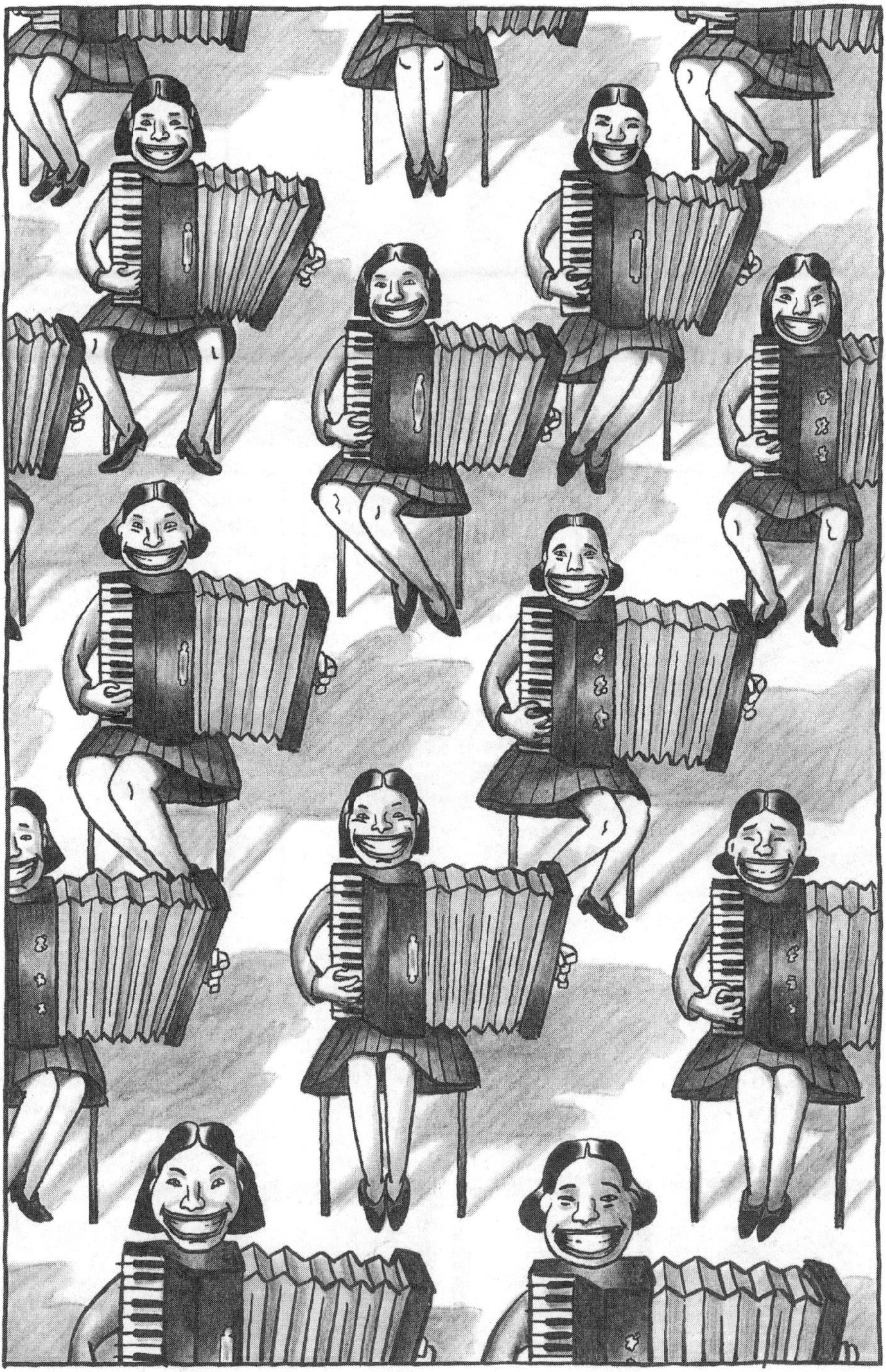

SUNDAYS, YOU CAN CHOOSE BETWEEN TWO CHANNELS. THE REST OF THE TIME THERE'S JUST ONE.

TONIGHT, THEY'RE SHOWING A DOCUMENTARY ABOUT EYE SURGERY.

IT'S OBVIOUSLY FROM ANOTHER COUNTRY — THE NETWORK LOGO IN THE CORNER OF THE SCREEN IS BLURRED AND INDECIPHERABLE.

THE NEWS IS NEXT. THE ANCHORWOMAN SPEAKS IN A TONE THAT'S BOTH EXALTED AND DELIBERATE, LIKE SHE'S BURYING A WAR HERO AT THE PANTHEON.

THE FIRST ITEM FEATURES ARCHIVAL FOOTAGE OF PAPA KIM VISITING A PLANT, AS THOUGH HE WERE STILL ALIVE.

NEXT UP IS TESTI- MONY BY RESISTANCE FIGHTERS WHO STRUGGLED AGAINST THE JAPANESE.

ALONG WITH PHOTOS OF SUMMARY EXECUTIONS CARRIED OUT BY THE OCCUPY- ING FORCES.

THEN KIM JR. IS SHOWN SPEAKING WITH PAPA KIM (AND FOR ONCE YOU SEE THE FATHER'S NECK TUMOR, WHICH IS USUALLY EDITED OUT OF PHOTOS).

146

IT ENDS ON AN ARTISTIC NOTE, WITH THE ARMY CHOIR SINGING ONE OF THE 6 OPERAS COMPOSED BY KIM JONG-IL.

THE EVENING WRAPS UP WITH AN EDIFYING FEATURE FILM: THE DESTINY OF A MEMBER OF THE SELF DEFENSE CORPS. YESTERDAY'S MOVIE WAS THE SONG OF CAMARADERIE, TOMORROW'S IS SEA OF BLOOD.

KNOCK KNOCK KNOCK

TONIGHT, DAVID AND I WANT TO GO TO THE DIPLOMATIC CLUB ON OUR OWN SO WE CAN SHOOT A GAME OF POOL WITHOUT OUR FAITHFUL SERVANTS.

IT'S THE FIRST TIME WE'VE GONE THIS FAR BY FOOT.

OH NO! RATS... IT'S SHUT.

DAMN.

HAVING COME ALL THIS WAY, WE DECIDE TO STOP BY THE KORYO FOR A DRINK WITH HENRI.

HE'S NOT THERE.

SHIT!

WHEN DAVID WAS HERE 5 YEARS AGO, YOU COULD TAKE A TAXI FROM ONE HOTEL TO ANOTHER WITHOUT A GUIDE OR TRANSLATOR.

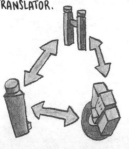

ONE TAXI, KORYO TO YANGGAKTO, PLEEZ

GUIDE?

FOR SOME REASON, THAT'S NO LONGER POSSIBLE.

FED UP.

AT NIGHT, THE STREETS ARE FULL OF PEOPLE MOVING ABOUT ON FOOT,

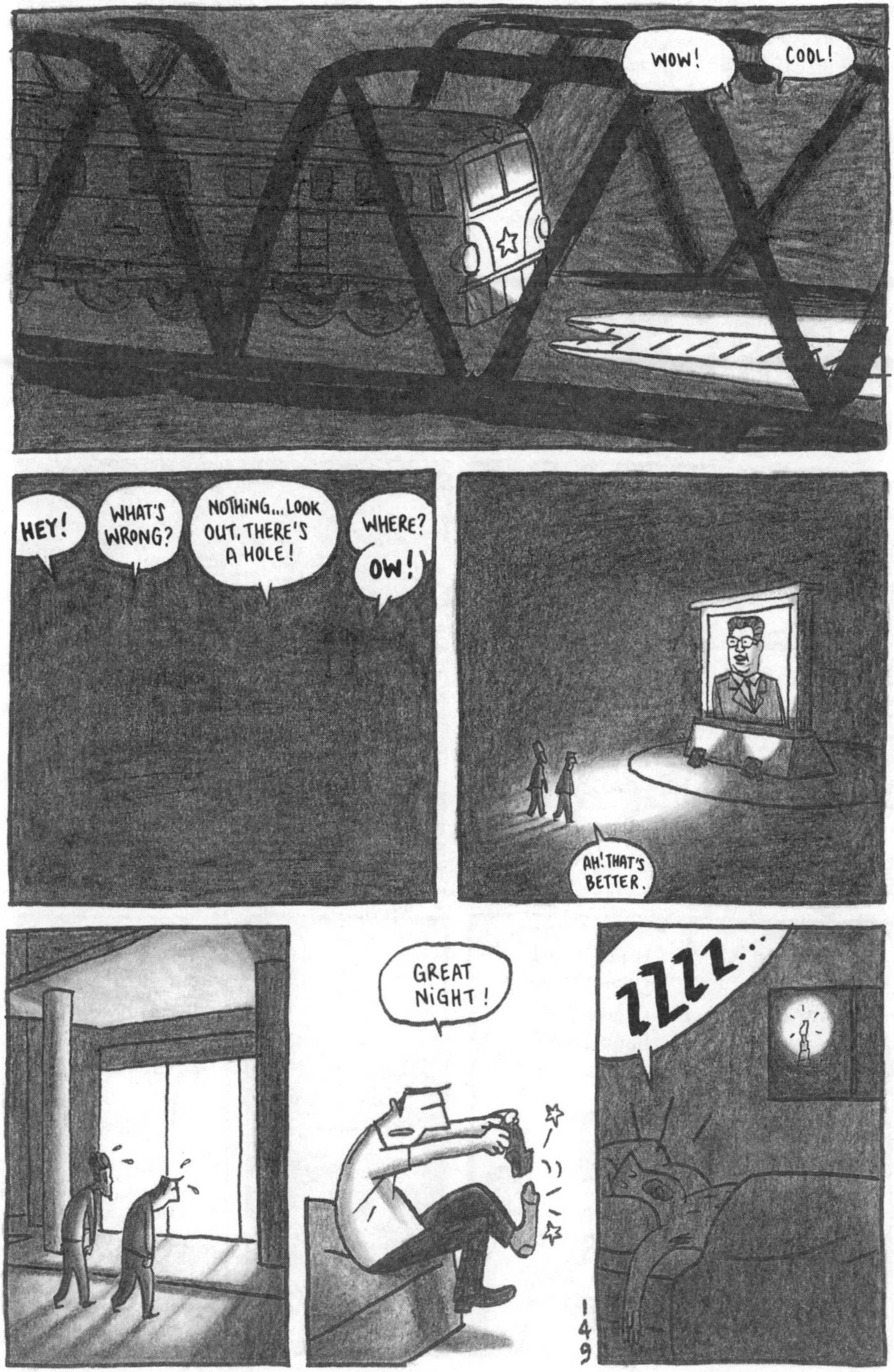
WOW!
COOL!
HEY!
WHAT'S WRONG?
NOTHING... LOOK OUT, THERE'S A HOLE!
WHERE?
OW!
AH! THAT'S BETTER.
GREAT NIGHT!
ZZZZ...

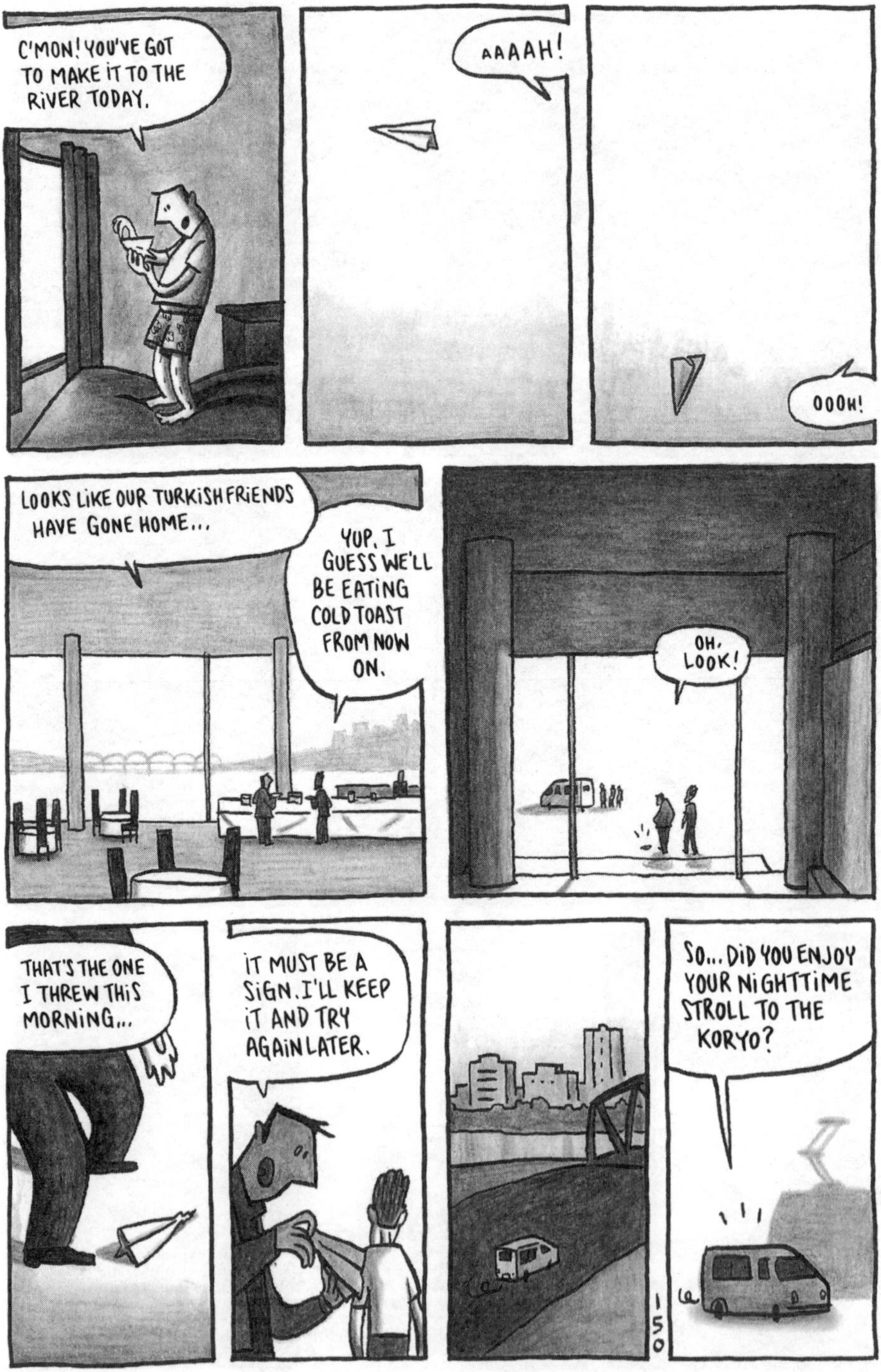
C'MON! YOU'VE GOT TO MAKE IT TO THE RIVER TODAY.
AAAAH!
OOOH!
LOOKS LIKE OUR TURKISH FRIENDS HAVE GONE HOME...
YUP, I GUESS WE'LL BE EATING COLD TOAST FROM NOW ON.
OH, LOOK!
THAT'S THE ONE I THREW THIS MORNING...
IT MUST BE A SIGN. I'LL KEEP IT AND TRY AGAIN LATER.
SO... DID YOU ENJOY YOUR NIGHTTIME STROLL TO THE KORYO?

WE GOT GOOD NEWS TODAY. THE DIRECTOR OF EPISODE 3 HAS BEEN FIRED.

A SHORT MAN WITH A LOUD VOICE AND A STRONG NORTHERN ACCENT (HE COMES FROM A VILLAGE NEAR THE CHINESE BORDER) IS TAKING OVER.

HE OBVIOUSLY MADE IT TO PYONGYANG ON THE MERITS OF HIS TALENT: HE HAS A GREAT SENSE OF MOVEMENT AND HIS WORK IS IMPECCABLE.

AND IN A WAY, I'M GLAD TO KNOW HIS DRAWING SKILLS LET HIM LEAVE HIS REMOTE VILLAGE TO MAKE A BETTER LIFE FOR HIMSELF AND HIS FAMILY.

COME TO THINK OF IT, IT'S PROBABLY THE ONLY UPSIDE TO THE WHOLE ASIAN SUBCONTRACTING SYSTEM.

THE OTHERS WHO WIND UP IN PYONGYANG TAKE A FAR LESS GLORIOUS PATH.

THE REGIME USES THIS FORM OF PROMOTION TO THANK ITS MOST ZEALOUS ELEMENTS IN THE PROVINCES, WHERE DENOUNCING NEIGHBORS IS ONE WAY OF GETTING NOTICED.

IT'S ESTIMATED THAT 50% OF THE PEOPLE HERE HAVE, AT SOME TIME OR ANOTHER, SERVED AS INFORMANTS.

QUIZ AMONG THESE VALOROUS CITIZENS LURK CONSPIRATORS WHO SEEK TO DESTABILIZE OUR GLORIOUS NATION...

Can you spot the traitors?

1 2 3 4 5 6 7

① BECAUSE HE LET THE PORTRAIT OF OUR DEAR LEADER GATHER DUST. ③ AND ④ BECAUSE THEY WEREN'T ENTHUSIASTIC ENOUGH AT THE LAST DEMONSTRATION. ⑤ AND ⑦ BECAUSE THEIR GRANDFATHERS FOUGHT WITH THE SOUTHERNERS IN 1951.

HEY... IT'S SO QUIET ALL OF A SUDDEN...

THERE'S NOT A SOUL ON THE FLOOR! I FINALLY FIND SOMEONE IN THE STAIRWELL.

WHERE ARE THEY?

AT THE MOVIE.

152

THE MOVIE?

ALL EMPLOYEES HAD BEEN INVITED TO A SCREENING OF THE LATEST MOVIE RELEASED BY THE ARMY'S STUDIO... IT'S NOT HARD TO GUESS WHAT IT WAS ABOUT.

모사령도

AND WHAT ABOUT YOU?

I DON'T LIKE MOVIES MADE HERE. THEY'RE BORING.

DURING MY ENTIRE STAY, THAT WAS THE MOST SUBVERSIVE THING I HEARD A NORTH KOREAN SAY.

AND GIVEN THE CONTEXT, HIS STATEMENT STRUCK ME AS INCREDIBLY BOLD.

SO, HOW WAS THE FLICK?

SUPER.

IT WAS ABOUT A RESISTANCE FIGHTER WHO LEAVES HIS VERY POOR FAMILY TO RISK HIS LIFE IN THE STRUGGLE AGAINST THE CAPITALIST ENEMY. HE COMES HOME WOUNDED TO...

153

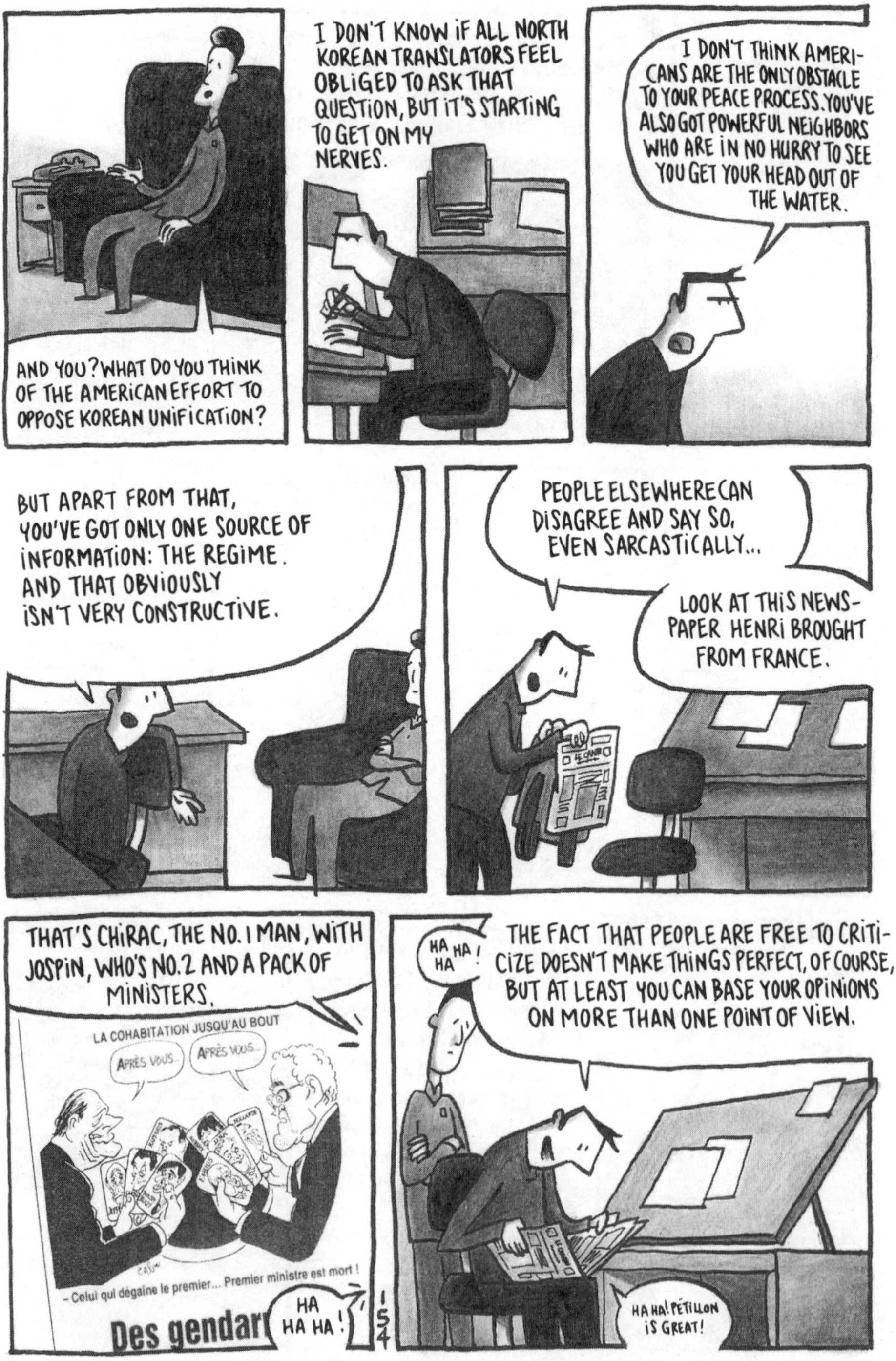
AND YOU? WHAT DO YOU THINK OF THE AMERICAN EFFORT TO OPPOSE KOREAN UNIFICATION?
I DON'T KNOW IF ALL NORTH KOREAN TRANSLATORS FEEL OBLIGED TO ASK THAT QUESTION, BUT IT'S STARTING TO GET ON MY NERVES.
I DON'T THINK AMERICANS ARE THE ONLY OBSTACLE TO YOUR PEACE PROCESS. YOU'VE ALSO GOT POWERFUL NEIGHBORS WHO ARE IN NO HURRY TO SEE YOU GET YOUR HEAD OUT OF THE WATER.
BUT APART FROM THAT, YOU'VE GOT ONLY ONE SOURCE OF INFORMATION: THE REGIME. AND THAT OBVIOUSLY ISN'T VERY CONSTRUCTIVE.
PEOPLE ELSEWHERE CAN DISAGREE AND SAY SO, EVEN SARCASTICALLY...
LOOK AT THIS NEWSPAPER HENRI BROUGHT FROM FRANCE.
THAT'S CHIRAC, THE NO. 1 MAN, WITH JOSPIN, WHO'S NO. 2 AND A PACK OF MINISTERS.
LA COHABITATION JUSQU'AU BOUT
APRÈS VOUS...
APRÈS VOUS...
– Celui qui dégaine le premier... Premier ministre est mort !
Des gendar
HA HA HA!
HA HA HA!
THE FACT THAT PEOPLE ARE FREE TO CRITICIZE DOESN'T MAKE THINGS PERFECT, OF COURSE, BUT AT LEAST YOU CAN BASE YOUR OPINIONS ON MORE THAN ONE POINT OF VIEW.
HA HA! PÉTILLON IS GREAT!

ACTUALLY, D'YOU KNOW WHAT WE SAY ABOUT DEMOCRACY AND DICTATORSHIP?

DICTATORSHIP MEANS SHUT UP, DEMOCRACY MEANS KEEP TALKING!

HA HA HA HA HA ! HA

MISTER GUY?

YES?

EN ROUTE TO ONE OF PYONGYANG'S CLASSIC TOURIST DESTINATIONS: THE CHILDREN'S PALACE. IT'S A KIND OF SCHOOL FOR THE COUNTRY'S MOST GIFTED CHILDREN.

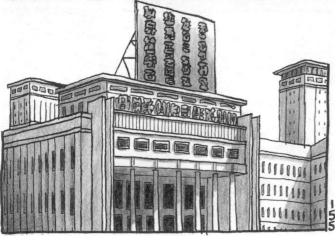

WHEN OUR DEAR LEADER KIM IL-SUNG CAME HERE, HE SAID "CHILDREN ARE THE TREASURE OF OUR NATION".

COMPUTERS, MUSIC, CALLIGRAPHY, EMBROIDERY ETC. WE GO FROM ONE ROOM TO THE NEXT, ALL FILLED WITH CHILDREN LABORING OVER ONE OF THESE DISCIPLINES.

WOW — 3DSMAX! I BET THEY DIDN'T BUY THE LICENSES...

"LONG LIVE OUR INVINCIBLE LEADER KIM JONG-IL"

THE MUSIC SECTION PRESENTS A LITTLE "IMPROVISED" CONCERT.

THE DEXTERITY OF THESE 8-YEAR OLD KIDS IS BREATHTAKING.

BUT BEHIND THEIR STRAINED FACES, YOU SENSE ALL THE CONCENTRATION THAT GOES INTO PLAYING THE MUSIC AND, ESPECIALLY INTO TRYING TO KEEP UP THOSE MISS WORLD SMILES.

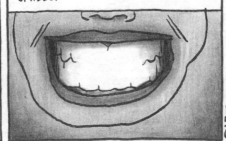

156

YOU CAN JUST IMAGINE THE TRAINING NEEDED TO ACHIEVE SUCH ROBOTIC RESULTS...

THE LITTLE SAVANT MONKEYS ARE DISPLAYED WITH GREAT PRIDE.

AS THOUGH THE THIN VENEER OF THEIR SMILES WERE PROOF THAT THESE YOUNG PRODIGIES ARE FLOURISHING HERE.

IT'S ALL SO COLD... AND SAD.

I COULD CRY.

THE VISIT ENDS IN A BIG AUDITORIUM, WHERE THE CHILDREN PERFORM A LIVELY SHOW.

THE FINAL CURTAIN FALLS WITH A PORTRAIT OF KIM JONG-IL IN ITS CENTER, AND ALL THE LITTLE ACTORS GREET IT WITH A DEEP BOW.

Our Father is Marshal Kim Il-Sung.
Our abode is the bosom of the Party.
We are brothers and sisters.
*We have nothing to envy in the world.**

HEY, THE STUDIO IS CLEARING OUT ITS BAGS OF RICE!

IT'S PAYDAY TODAY.

* EXCERPT FROM A POEM IN THE CHILDREN'S PALACE ENTITLED: *WE ARE THE HAPPIEST CHILDREN IN THE WORLD.*

THE EMPLOYEES ARE PAID A SALARY, OF COURSE, BUT GIVEN THE FREQUENT FOOD SHORTAGES, THE STUDIO ALSO STORES AND REDISTRIBUTES RICE.

HMM... BUT WHERE'S THE RICE FROM?...

BAGS OF RICE... THERE CAN HARDLY BE A BETTER WAY TO KEEP SUBCONTRACTING PRODUCTIVE.

HERE I AM, WORKING FOR FRANCE'S BIGGEST TELEVISION NETWORK.

TONIGHT, CAPTAIN SIN GETS STUCK JOINING ME ON THE WAY HOME.

AS USUAL, IT'S AN OPPORTUNITY TO FIND OUT MORE ABOUT THIS ENIGMATIC COUNTRY.

SO, HOW WAS THE ARMY?

NORTH KOREA HAS THE WORLD'S 4TH LARGEST ARMY, WITH OVER A MILLION SOLDIERS AND UP TO 4 MILLION RESERVISTS ON CALL. IT ALSO HAS:

2000 TANKS STATIONED ALONG ITS BORDER.

600 MISSILES, INCLUDING SCUDS, NO DONG MISSILES (THE NATION'S PRIDE) AND THE TAEPO DONG, WHICH WAS TESTED OVER JAPAN IN 1998.

AT LEAST 4000 TONS OF BIOCHEMICAL WEAPONS.

A NUCLEAR PROGRAM SHROUDED IN MYSTERY, THE BETTER TO CASH IN ON ITS DESTRUCTIVE CAPACITY.

DURING AN ANNUAL WEEKLONG MANEUVER, ALL CITIZENS ARE EXPECTED TO BE READY TO PUT ON GEAR AND ASSEMBLE IN THE BIG SQUARE AT THE SOUND OF A SIREN.

AND SINCE THE HIERARCHIES IN CIVILIAN LIFE EXTEND TO THOSE IN THE ARMY, CAPTAIN SIN, FOR EXAMPLE, WOULD HEAD A BATTALION OF ANIMATORS.

VOILÀ! I'VE DRAWN A PLAN OF THE POSITION WE'RE GOING TO ATTACK!

THE PERSPECTIVE SEEMS OFF, SIR!

HE'S RIGHT! THE FARTHER THINGS ARE, THE SMALLER THEY HAVE TO BE, SIR!

IT'S ALL WRONG.

LOOK AT THAT TANK MOVE... THE WEIGHT! THE INERTIA! IT'S AMAZING!

THOSE BASTARDS REALLY KNOW WHEN TO SQUASH AND STRETCH!

HEH HEH!

WHAT?

OH, NOTHING.

IT'S NGO FRIDAY, AND WE HUSTLE A LIFT FROM AN ACQUAINTANCE AT THE HOTEL RESTAURANT.

EVERYONE'S THERE AND IT'S A PARTY.

ROBERTA IS BACK FROM A FEW DAYS IN BEIJING. FROM HERE, CHINA LOOKS LIKE A HAVEN OF LIBERTY.

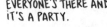

BY THE END, THERE'S NO ONE LEFT TO DRIVE US.

RICHARD AND I ARE GIVEN SHEETS AND CUSHIONS, AND WE WIND UP AT TIM'S – A BRIT WHO'S AS DRUNK AS WE ARE.

HE KICKS US OUT AT THE CRACK OF DAWN TO GO INSPECT A NORTHERN VILLAGE WITH HIS TRANSLATOR.

SITTING ON SWINGS, WE WONDER HOW LIKELY WE ARE TO FIND A WAY HOME.

A DIPLOMAT WHO LOOKS VAGUELY FAMILIAR STOPS HIS CAR AND WALKS OVER.

WE'RE OUT OF LUCK. HE JUST WANTS SOMEONE TO BUY HIS FRIDGE AND TV.

160

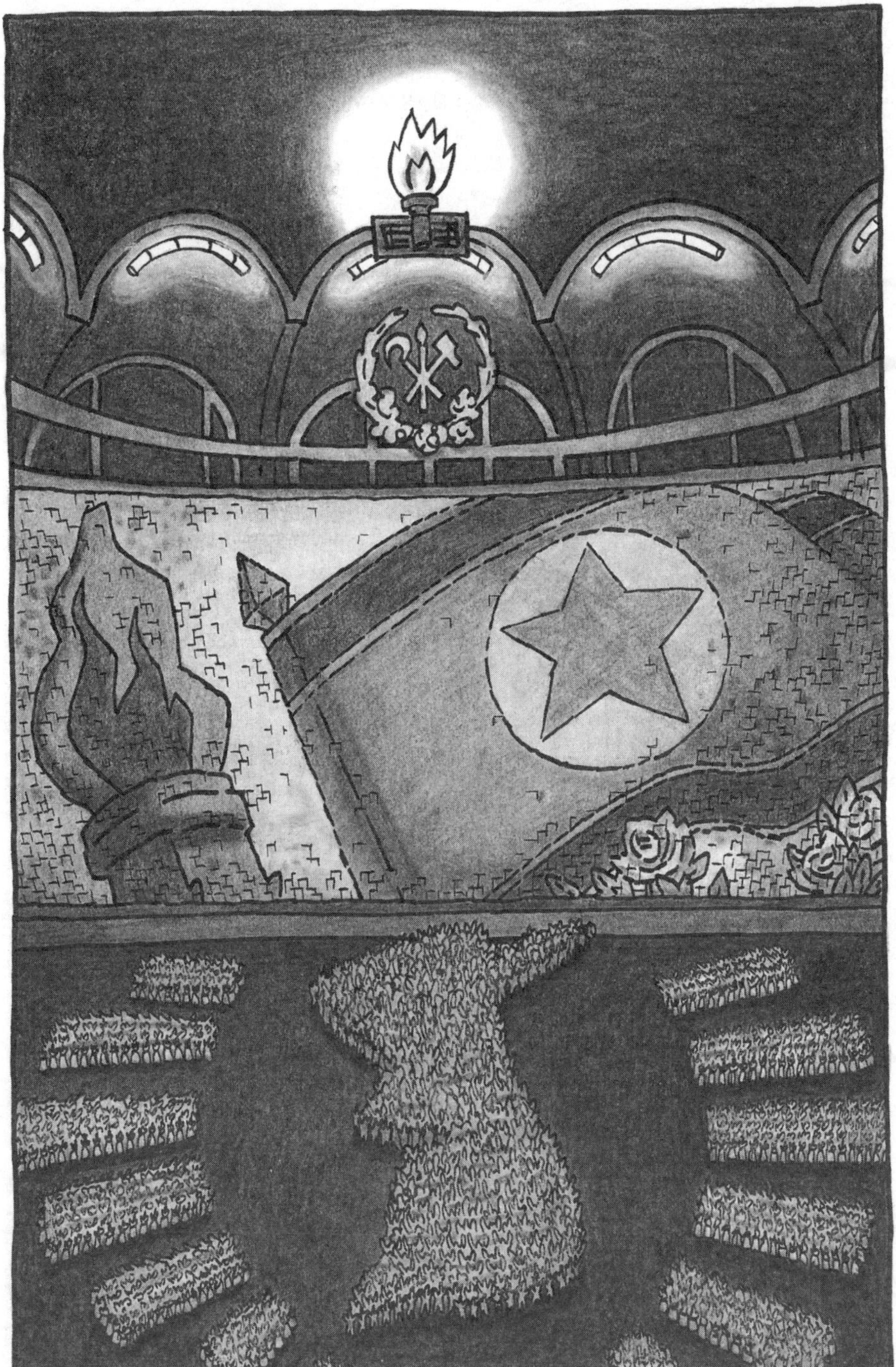

KNOCK KNOCK KNOCK

FOR A REASON THAT'S BEYOND ME, WE HAVE TO BE AT THE STUDIO EARLY TODAY TO WRAP UP AN EPISODE.

YOU'VE GOT TO BE KIDDING.

THE HALLWAYS ARE EMPTY, BUT A LARGE GROUP OF EMPLOYEES IS IN THE CONFERENCE ROOM, LISTENING TO A MAN I RECOGNIZE AS THE SUPPOSED DIRECTOR WHO'S ALWAYS AROUND.

A RADIO ON THE WALL OF EVERY ROOM (I'D NEVER NOTICED IT BEFORE) IS ALTERNATING BETWEEN SPEECHES AND MUSIC.

I SWITCH IT OFF.

OH, SHUT UP!

CLICK

162

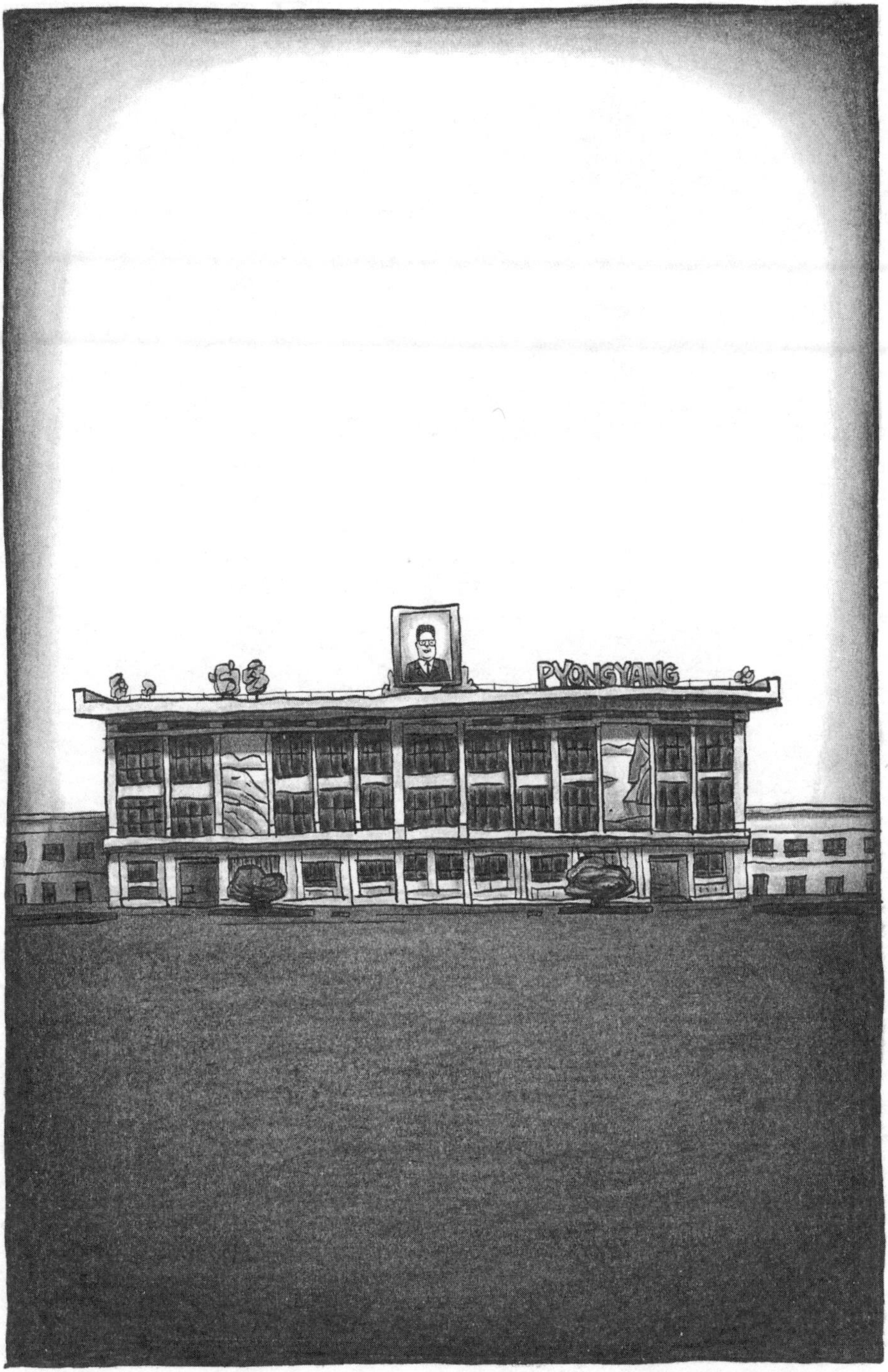
PYONGYANG

A SINGLE SHOE STYLE, IN A CHOICE OF RED OR BLUE, CAN TAKE UP MOST OF A DEPARTMENT.

IT'S LIKE LOOKING AT AN INSTALLATION IN A CONTEMPORARY ART MUSEUM.

HEY!

KIDS CARRYING BUCKETS OF WATER...

WHAT'RE THEY DOING?

THEY'RE WATERING THE GRASS...

... FOR FUN.

I SEE...

AFTER MONTHS OF RENOVATION, RESTAURANT NO. 3 IS FINALLY OPENING TONIGHT.

HEY! THAT'S GREAT NEWS!

IT'S A HUGE EVENT IN OUR LITTLE UNIVERSE. THE MONOTONOUS MENU AT RESTAURANT NO. I HAS BEEN DOWN TO A STRICT MINIMUM LATELY.

CARROT SALAD?

NO.

TO CELEBRATE, WE'VE INVITED FABRICE. HE'S REPLACING RICHARD, WHO LEFT THIS WEEK ALONG WITH HENRI.

THEY TRANSFERRED PART OF THE NO. I MENU TO NO. 3.

NO WAY.

CARROT SALAD?

YES.

THOSE CROOKS.

I END THE EVENING WITH FABRICE, TELLING HIM ABOUT MY STAY.

EVER SEEN THE "REVERSE"?

THREE MONTHS LATER, WHEN WE MEET AGAIN IN PARIS, IT'S HIS TURN TO DO THE TELLING.

ARE YOU KIDDING? WHAT A JOKE!

HEY, IF I DO A BOOK ABOUT MY STAY IN KOREA, MAYBE YOU COULD DRAW THAT ONE FOR ME...

JUST 2 PAGES, NO MORE.

My outings with Kim were starting to weigh on me. I couldn't get an unfiltered view of the country. I finally hit on a plan.

Sundays, I pretended to stay at the hotel. My guide backed off a bit, and I slipped out on my own. But the night before I left...

Fabrice, I have something very important to tell you.

the house where Kim was born

The Spy ship

The mountains

The Juche tower

The War memorial

The Museum of the horrors of war

etc...

I'd been seen the day before in a neighborhood that wasn't up to revolutionary standards, photographing a pile of garbage cans.

It's forbidden. Garbage is not a good souvenir of North Korea. There are so many beautiful things to photograph.

I'd been warned once before, when we mistakenly found ourselves in a provincial shantytown.

NO

The message had been clear.

The problem was, I didn't know what garbage he was talking about.

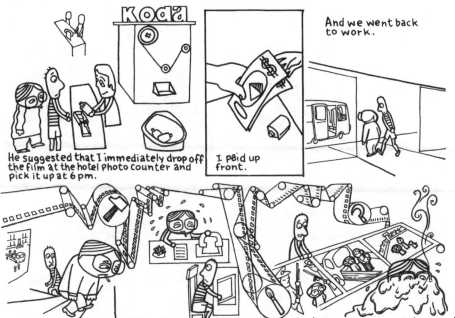

He suggested that I immediately drop off the film at the hotel photo counter and pick it up at 6 pm.

I paid up front.

And we went back to work.

Watching Kim go to pieces that afternoon, I got a sense of the danger my benign photos posed for him. I tried to talk to him, but he shut down completely. I imagined the worst. Horror films played out in both of our minds.

At 6 pm we picked up the negatives. Kim took them and disappeared upstairs.

He was gone for almost an hour.

When he came back, he was relieved: There was no garbage on the negatives. But a few shots were scratched out...

I exploded into a rage that was as sudden as it was inappropriate. "Somebody buy new glasses for the spies! I've been humiliated!" As though I was the one who had been in danger.

The last supper with the team was a glum affair.

Strangely enough, nobody asked for any of the other films I'd shot while I was there.

IT'S ALWAYS INTERESTING TO GET ANOTHER PERSPECTIVE ON THINGS!

THAT'S WHAT CAPTAIN SIN SAID BEFORE TAKING ME TO SEE THE MUSEUM OF IMPERIALIST OCCUPATION.

I WAS GOING TO GET MY HAIR CUT.

I TRIED TO TALK MY WAY OUT OF IT, BUT THEY REMINDED ME HOW HARD IT IS TO GET A SUNDAY DRIVING PASS.

AMERICANS ARE OUR SWORN ENEMIES.

AND TO SHOW HOW MONSTROUS THEY ARE, THE MUSEUM DOCUMENTS ALL ATROCITIES COMMITED BY AMERICANS AGAINST THE KOREAN PEOPLE DURING THE WAR.

168

THERE ARE NO HALF-MEASURES: THE INVENTORY INCLUDES EVERY FORM OF TORTURE FROM THE INQUISITION TO THE THIRD REICH.

THE RACK
NEEDLES UNDER THE NAILS.
CREMATORIUM

A NUMBER OF HORRIFYING PAINTINGS DRIVE HOME THE MESSAGE.

SOLDIERS FORCING CHILDREN TO DRINK MOTOR OIL.

SOLDIERS NAILING ANTI-AMERICAN PROPAGANDA TO THE AUTHOR'S FOREHEAD.

SOLDIERS TRYING TO FORCE A RESISTANCE FIGHTER TO TALK. UNSUCCESSFULLY, OF COURSE

IT GOES ON LIKE THAT FOR TWO CRAMMED FLOORS.

OUR GUIDE IS TRULY STUNNING, AND LISTENING TO HER GRAPHIC DESCRIPTIONS, I THINK UP A FEW TORTURES OF MY OWN THAT I WOULDN'T MIND INFLICTING ON HER.

ONCE THE VISIT IS OVER, THE GUIDE ASKS ME A QUESTION THAT IS DISCONCERTINGLY NAIVE.

WHAT DO YOU THINK OF AMERICANS NOW?

169

I DON'T THINK WAR IS EVER "CLEAN", NO MATTER WHO'S FIGHTING. AND I CERTAINLY WOULDN'T DEMONIZE AN ENTIRE PEOPLE ON THE BASIS OF 3 BLURRY PHOTOS AND A FEW PAINTINGS.

WHAT ELSE!

I THINK THAT SPEECH IS THE REASON I WASN'T INVITED A WEEK LATER TO THE ANNUAL ANTI-IMPERIALIST CELEBRATION, WHERE PEOPLE IN THE CROWD ARE TURNED INTO HUMAN PIXELS TO CREATE MURALS TO THE GLORY OF THE NATION.

BACK IN THE CAR, MY COMRADES HAVE A LITTLE SULK.

WE GO TO A PARK FOR A PICNIC. ON THE MENU: MARINATED MEAT (TRANSPORTED IN A PLASTIC BAG) THAT WE'LL GRILL ON A GAS COOKER.

OUT OF CURIOSITY, I HAVE A LOOK.

UGHHH.

AND DESPITE MYSELF, I SAY:

HEY! THAT'S JUST LIKE THE MUSEUM!

? Mm. m' m'

OOPS!

HA HA! HA HA HA HA!

I'D NEVER SEEN THEM LAUGH SO HARD.

1 7 0

THANKS TO THE BOOZE, WE END THE DAY SINGING.

STAND UP, ALL VICTIMS OF OPPRESSION* FOR THE TYRANTS FEAR YOUR MIGHT*

* SIN CAN SING THE INTERNATIONALE IN 4 LANGUAGES, INCLUDING 2 HE DOESN'T SPEAK!

MY HEAD FEELS LIKE MUSH TODAY.

Ow!

WE CELEBRATED DAVID'S DEPARTURE LAST NIGHT AND I HAD ONE DRINK TOO MANY.

LUCKILY, I'VE HAD LESS WORK TO DO SINCE THE ARRIVAL OF OUR NEW DIRECTOR.

AH! VERY NICE.

MY LAST WEEK IS AS CALM AS COULD BE.

WHERE HAS THAT TRANSLATOR GONE?

EXCEPT FOR ONE INCIDENT.

THERE YOU ARE!

I'D LIKE TO GO BACK TO STORE Nº 1 TO BUY A TOY FOR MY GODSON.

SURE. I'LL BE RIGHT BACK.

HALF AN HOUR LATER.

WHAT THE HELL IS HE UP TO?

EXASPERATED AT HAVING TO ACCOUNT FOR EVERY SINGLE OUTING...

... I DECIDE TO GO ON MY OWN.

NO ONE TAKES NOTICE OF ME. IT'S STRANGE. I FEEL INVISIBLE, EVEN THOUGH A FOREIGNER ON THE STREETS OF PYONGYANG IS NO ORDINARY SIGHT.

IF ANYONE DID TALK TO ME, THEY'D PROBABLY BE VIEWED AS SUSPECT. SO LOOKING THE OTHER WAY IS PROBABLY THE SAFEST THING TO DO.

AW.

I DON'T FIND ANYTHING I LIKE.

BY THE TIME I GET BACK, MY TRANSLATOR IS A WRECK. HE'S LOOKED EVERYWHERE FOR ME.

"LUCKILY YOU DIDN'T HAVE A CAMERA", HE SAYS, HIS VOICE TREMBLING.

FROM THAT MOMENT TO THE END OF MY STAY, HE STICKS TO MY HEELS.

MISTER GUY, DO YOU LIKE MOVIES?

172

THAT DEPENDS.

WOULD YOU LIKE TO SEE THE NATIONAL STUDIO?

LET'S GO!

KIM JONG-IL HAS HONORED OUR STUDIO WITH HIS PRESENCE 320 TIMES AND SUPERVISED NO LESS THAN 1000 FILMS.

THE FILM SETS ARE OVER HERE.

A VAST CHOICE OF PERIODS AND LOCATIONS ARE AVAILABLE TO DIRECTORS.

THERE'S THE PERIOD BEFORE, DURING OR JUST AFTER THE JAPANESE OCCUPATION, AND THE SAME THING AGAIN FOR THE KOREAN WAR.

AND WHAT DO YOU DO FOR SCIENCE FICTION?

AT THE END, WE'RE SHOWN EXCERPTS OF THEIR LATEST PRODUCTIONS.

EXCERPT ①: UNDER JAPANESE OCCUPATION, A KOREAN BEGGAR IS BEATEN BY JAPANESE SOLDIERS.

EXCERPT ②: IN A JAPANESE LABOR CAMP, A DETAINEE HAS HIS TONGUE CUT OUT FOR REFUSING TO APOLOGIZE.

EXCERPT ③: SURROUNDED, A NORTH KOREAN SOLDIER SETS FIRE TO HIS HOME INSTEAD OF CAPITULATING TO CAPITALISTS.

KIM JONG-IL LOVES THE MOVIES!

LOVES THE MOVIES! HIS FAVORITE FILM IS FRIDAY THE 13TH.

THAT'S ACCORDING TO REVELATIONS MADE BY SOUTH KOREAN FILMMAKER SHIN SANK-OK AFTER HE EMERGED FROM HIS EXTRAORDINARY ADVENTURE:

IN 1978, NORTH KOREAN AGENTS KIDNAPPED HIM. HE FOUND HIMSELF IN PYONGYANG WHERE KIM JONG-IL INVITED HIM TO PRODUCE FILMS. HE REFUSED, TRIED TO ESCAPE AND LANDED IN JAIL.

FOUR YEARS OF INCARCERATION LATER, HE PLAYED ALONG, PRODUCING A TOTAL OF SIX FILMS. DURING A TRIP ABROAD, HE MANAGED TO ESCAPE AFTER EIGHT YEARS OF CAPTIVITY.

MY FAREWELL DINNER, LIKE ALL THE OTHERS, IS HELD IN RESTAURANT No. 1.

WHEN I LEFT FOR NORTH KOREA, I WAS TOLD TO TAKE ALONG A GIFT FOR THE PRESIDENT OF THE ANIMATION STUDIO.

OH WELL, I NEVER DID RUN INTO HIM.

IN THE 1990s, AT THE HEIGHT OF A FAMINE THAT CLAIMED SOME 2 MILLION LIVES, NORTH KOREA WAS THE WORLD'S BIGGEST CLIENT FOR HENESSY COGNAC.

LET'S REDISTRIBUTE THE WEALTH TO THE MASSES.

TOC TOC

CAPTAIN SIN?

OH! VSOP HENNESSY!

FOR YOU.

THANK YOU!

ONE OF THE FEW MOMENTS OF REAL JOY I WITNESSED.

WELL, THERE GOES TWO MONTHS OF LOYAL SERVICE.

SCENE 327
DIALOGUE: GRANDFATHER
-BYE BYE LITTLE BEARS!
C'MON! GO!
DELISLE